Print & Pattern Kids
Bowie Style

Published in 2013 by

Laurence King Publishing Ltd
361–373 City Road
London EC1V 1LR
United Kingdom
Tel: +44 20 7841 6900
Fax: +44 20 7841 6910
email: enquiries@laurenceking.com
www.laurenceking.com

A catalogue record for this book
is available from the British Library.

ISBN 978-1-78067300-4

Book and cover design: & SMITH
www.andsmithdesign.com
Senior Editor: Sophie Wise
Printed in China.

PRINT & PATTERN KIDS

Contents

Introduction
Marie Perkins

a.k.a. Bowie Style

www.printpattern.blogspot.com

Within the world of design, I find I am continually drawn to patterns and illustrations created for children. And so, it would seem, are many other creatives. Perhaps it is the boldness of the colours or the graphic simplicity of the motifs, but many a designer will be attracted to this fun and expressive genre. Legendary graphic designer Paul Rand, well-known for his posters and logos, relished the work he created for children's books in the late 1950s. He felt it gave him a welcome respite from the constraints of corporate work.

For children, especially those who may not have yet fully developed their literacy skills, imagery is everything. In their early, formative years their decor, clothing and books will be their introduction to the visual arts. With this in mind, parents naturally want to surround their children with fun and stimulating design, which has created a fantastic market for designers and illustrators working today.

Here we have gathered together just over 100 individuals and companies to celebrate the wonderful creativity that is available in this market. We showcase the skills of designers who can distil complex ideas, objects, animals and themes into images children can identify with and understand.

We asked all of our contributors which designers and illustrators have most inspired them. I hope this will give you a great insight into their influences and perhaps introduce you to new artists you weren't aware of and whom you may want to research for yourself.

Many of the individual designers featured are freelancers and would be absolutely delighted to receive commissions or licensing enquiries.

Marie Perkins

Akemi Tezuka

www.asterisk-agency.com
info@asterisk-agency.com

weather forecast

01 // Akemi Tezuka is a designer and illustrator based in Tokyo, Japan. Akemi studied Graphic Design in the Industrial Design Faculty at Joshi Bijutsu University. Her clients have included Pie Books, Kokuyo S&T, Benesse Corporation, Gakken Holdings, and Kumon Publishing. 'My main inspirations for my works are the design elements in screen structures,' Akemi says. Her dream commission would be to write and illustrate a book that appealed to both adults and children. In the future Akemi hopes to illustrate books for a publishing company that will 'keep reprinting for decades'.

Design Hero: Olle Eksell

Favourite Children's Illustrators:
Alain Grée (see pages 10–15),
Ed Emberley (see pages 104–9)

Top / Weather Forecast
Proportion and balance are used to great effect in this composition, which could be best described as cheerful, thanks to the character's beaming smile. The very tall hat and outstretched arm create the structure but also add a humorous, whimsical touch.

Bottom / Squirrels
Two adorable squirrels, made even cuter by their neckerchiefs, gather nuts using spoons. The French text, which has been very cleverly placed in the negative space left by the spoons, refers to 'harvest fruits'.

Opposite / Connect
When examined closely, Akemi's illustrations have a stippled texture that looks like traditional airbrushing. In fact, Akemi uses Adobe Photoshop to do all her work, and all her works done prior to digital, such as watercolours or designs created using other techniques, have been kept as stock. In this design different people from around the globe are invited to connect.

Alain Grée

www.alaingree.com
www.ricobel.com
ricobel.japan@gmail.com

02 // Legendary author and illustrator Alain Grée was born in 1936 in Eaubonne, France. He studied in Paris at the Ecole des Arts Appliqués and the Ecole Nationale Supérieure des Beaux-Arts and after graduation decided to become a freelance author and illustrator so that he could sail around the world on his boat. His work is renowned for its romantic and idealized representation of childhood and the exciting new world that was emerging in the 1960s. His timeless, colourful and sunny style not only appeals to children but also to adults who appreciate his design skill and enjoy the nostalgia. His books have been translated into 20 different languages around the world and he has also worked on children's games and magazines. Grée recently remastered some of his earlier children's books for the Japanese publisher Geneon Entertainment Inc. and is now working closely together with RicoBel to develop the licensing of his work further throughout the world.

Favourite Children's Illustrators: Alice and Martin Provensen

Top / In a Car
© Alain Grée & RicoBel. From the 1968 book *I Know About Cars*.

Bottom / Mini Austin
© Alain Grée & RicoBel. From the 1968 Casterman-published book *L'Automobile*.

Opposite top / Birds on a Wire
© Alain Grée & RicoBel. From the 1968 book *I Know About Counting*.

Opposite bottom / Children Eating
© Alain Grée & RicoBel. Charming illustration of happy children sitting at the table.

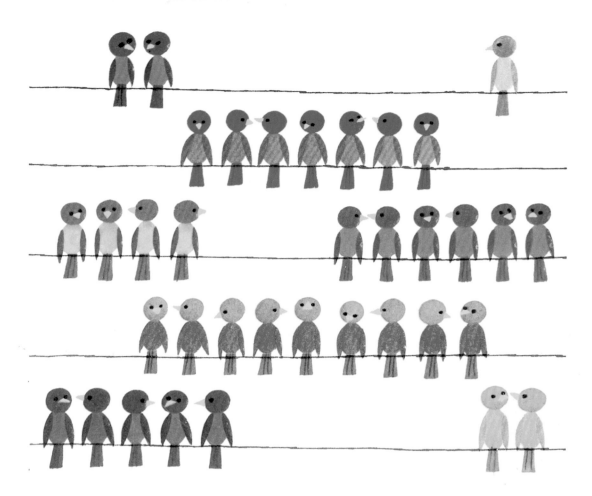

Top / There is a...
© Alain Grée & RicoBel. The '*There is a...*' series of books was originally created between 1966–7 and published by Hachette. The books have been re-released in Japanese by RicoBel.

Bottom / Schoolbus with Pilou and Romeo.
© Alain Grée & RicoBel. Reproduced by RicoBel as a postcard, this illustration originally featured in the book *I Know About Travel*.

Opposite / Animals
© Alain Grée & RicoBel. Alain wanted to make his animal illustrations 'cute and friendly so they would be loved by everyone'. Capucine the fox was an important Alain Grée character as a loyal friend to Pilou.

DANSE, JOLIE DANSE Nº 4

Above / Jolie Danse
© Alain Grée & RicoBel. A sleeve design for a 1960s children's record called Jolie Danse No.4.

Opposite / Au Jardin Cover
© Alain Grée & RicoBel. *The Garden*, published in 1968 by Casterman, was one of the 'Achille et Bergamote' series of books about an inseparable brother and sister who never run out of the enthusiasm to learn. The series ran from 1962–83.

ALAIN GRÉE

au jardin

CASTERMAN

Albert + Marie

www.albertandmarie.com
www.etsy.com/shop/AlbertandMarie
hi.albertandmarie@gmail.com

03 // Albert + Marie is a husband and wife design/print duo. Will Ecke and Liz Doering established Albert + Marie in San Francisco, California, in 2010 for the 'purpose of making cute things'. Liz is originally from Minnesota and Will is from Wisconsin and together they collaborate on ideas and certain aspects of each project. Will tends to do the design, and Liz the printing and operations. Will works for a small design boutique in San Francisco, where his designs tend to be mostly illustrative. Liz is a freelance creative producer and handles all things operational and logistical. A lot of their inspiration comes from the 1960s, especially the hand-drawn and illustrative themes in advertising and in children's books. Liz and Will find there is something distinctive and charming in the way things used to be drawn in the '60s, and before. It can be abstract, or it can be really sweet. Liz and Will are hoping to continue to design lots of prints and posters for Albert + Marie in the near future, and would love to start writing children's books that they can then illustrate! They are also open to custom assignments and freelance commissions.

Design Heroes: Olle Eksell, Paul Rand, Hervlustrate

Favourite Children's Illustrators: Mary Blair, Tove Jansson, Marc Boutavant (see pages 196–9)

1/75

1/75

albert + marie

1 / 75

Opposite & above / Fish + Seal, Kitty + Citrus, Leaf + Butterfly
All from the 'Up in the Air' series of handmade screen-prints
created for the Albert + Marie Etsy shop. A few years ago
lots of Will and Liz's friends were having children; two of
the new arrivals – Otto and Emma – inspired them to create
Albert + Marie.

albert & marie

1/75

1 / 75

Alice Apple

www.aliceapple.co.uk
www.aliceapple.etsy.com
aliceeburrows@yahoo.co.uk

04 // Alice Burrows has been designing and making under the label Alice Apple since 2008. Originally from Shropshire, Alice now lives in Totnes, South Devon, with her partner, son, and little twin daughters. Alice studied Textile Design at the University of Derby, where she specialized in print and graduated in 2001. Since then she has done work for The Art Group, had a set of three posters for sale in Habitat, and designed babywear prints for companies Organic Monkey and Cheeks and Cherries. Alice continues to design her own surface patterns and toys, which are sold online and in various international independent shops. Since Alice had children they have had a strong influence on her work, and she has a passion for bright colour and bold imagery with a strong take on the 1960s and '70s. For ideas she often refers to vintage craft books, children's books, and her main interest: 1970s fabric design. Alice's ambition would be to design a range of homeware, for children or grown-ups, for a store such as Heal's or Habitat. But she is also very grateful for being able to do what she loves: selling and making her own creations.

Design Heroes: Graziela Preiser, Orla Kiely (see pages 232–3), Sanna Anukka

Favourite Children's Illustrators: Fiep Westendorp, Dick Bruna, David McKee

Opposite top / Soft Toy Blocks
Alice designed and illustrated all the sides of these
children's building blocks which were then digitally
printed onto fabric. They were then cut, sewn,
and filled with foam cubes to make them safe
for babies right from birth. Sold in her Etsy shop.

Opposite bottom /
Dutch Gables Houses and Doll Friends
A selection of Alice's handmade toys and
cushions from her Etsy shop. The Dutch houses
are inspired by the fact that Alice is half Dutch.

Above / Apple Doll
A super-sweet doll illustrated with a retro girl by
Alice. Digitally printed onto fabric, and then hand-
sewn to create a toy for sale in her Etsy shop.

Above / Family
Alice designed a doll's house cushion and then created a fantastic retro family to go with it. Printed onto fabric to make into soft toys.

Opposite top / Summer Tulips
Here Alice has pared the form of the tulip flower down to its barest essence to make a striking print which also features a beautifully selected colour palette. Sold as fabric in Alice's Spoonflower shop: *www.spoonflower. com/profiles/aliceapple*.

Opposite bottom left / Elephant Block
This elephant has been rendered with very clean lines and minimal detail but is still recognizable. Original digital design for printing onto fabric to make into soft foam cubes for babies' toys.

Opposite bottom right / Boy Block
Alice's aesthetic runs through all her work, paring down this illustration of a boy to its simplest forms. A digital design for printing onto fabric to make into soft block toys.

Amy Mullen

www.mintparcel.com
amymullen.carbonmade.com

05 // Amy Mullen grew up in Pennsylvania and currently lives in Arlington, Virginia. Amy originally studied a BA in Dance, but feels she is visually inclined by nature and is self-taught in the field of digital illustration. Amy created the label Mint Parcel for her work and produces prints and illustrations, which she describes as 'all things cute, simple and sweet'. She writes and illustrates picture books, and finds children's books are her greatest inspiration. Clients have included *Babiekins Magazine*. For her future ambition, Amy would love to be illustrating/designing/picture-book-writing full-time.

Design Hero: Chip Kidd

Favourite Children's Illustrators: Hilary Knight, Oliver Jeffers, Jen Corace

Top / Sweet Houses
Everything within this digital illustration has been created with either a rectangle, circle or triangle, with great effect.

Bottom / Little Astronaut
Space, astronauts, and rockets are a popular theme for boys. But in Amy's hands the emphasis is on cute and retro charm.

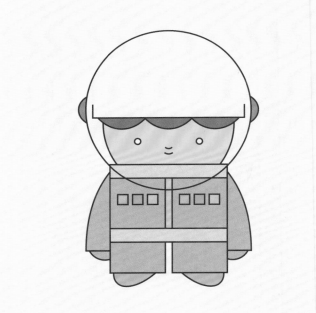

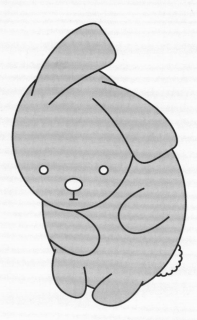

Amy Schimler

www.amyschimler.com
www.childrensillustrators.com/amyschimler
amy@amyschimler.com

o6 // Amy Schimler is originally from New York but now lives in Atlanta, Georgia. She studied Textile Design at the Rhode Island School of Design (RISD) and Fibre Arts and Painting at the Massachusetts College of Art. Amy finds inspiration for her work in nature, vintage textiles, and children's drawings. Her own son Zach's artwork has been a huge inspiration: 'He drew the happiest dinosaurs I have ever seen'. Amy's client list includes Target, Baby Gap, American Greetings, Hallmark, Papyrus, Fisher Price, Pottery Barn for Kids and Babies R Us. Amy finds it a joy to illustrate for all aspects of the children's market and would love to illustrate and publish more children's books.

Design Heroes: Fujiwo Ishimoto, Milton Avery, Maira Kalman

Favourite Children's Illustrators: Ezra Keats, Melissa Sweet, Brian Wildsmith

Above / Tree Garden
Amy uses abstracted trees and stylized rainbows to create a magical landscape in this print licensed by Robert Kaufman Fabrics.

Opposite / Animal Alphabet
A portfolio piece Amy created to demonstrate her fabulous skill at illustrating animals. The additional type is educational and adds style.

Overleaf left / Dog Toss
This scattered design, known as a 'toss', features a variety of dogs playing with balls, which gives it a lovely sense of movement. Licensed by Robert Kaufman Fabrics.

Overleaf right / Patterned Elephants
A portfolio piece featuring elephants enlivened with different infill patterns and textures.

Amy Wilde

www.landofthecuckoo.blogspot.co.uk
amy_wilde@hotmail.com

07 // Amy Wilde is based in Bradford, West Yorkshire, in the UK. She studied Graphic Design at the University of Teesside, Middlesbrough, and has been a designer in the greetings cards industry for eight years. In this time she has designed for Hallmark and most major high street and grocery stores in the UK, such as Next, Asda, Tesco, John Lewis, Waitrose, BHS, Sainsbury's, and a number of charity stores including Oxfam and Cancer Research. Amy has been lucky enough to work in some very creative studio environments and meet some lovely, talented designer friends, like Rachael Taylor, along the way, who have given her inspiration. Her daughter's fun and colourful personality also feeds its way into her work and she thinks you have to be 'a big kid at heart to design children's characters every day.' Amy's dream commission would be to write and design her very own children's picture book or to have her characters turned into animation.

Design Heroes: Rachael Taylor, Gemma Corell, Ben Javens

Favourite Children's Illustrators: Oliver Jeffers, Neal Layton, Russell Ayto

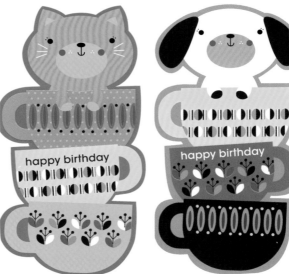

Top / Woo Hoo Panda
A lovely grey paper background sets off the black and white graphic panda perfectly. The cheerful colour is provided by the typography and the oversized panda's head gives it a whimsical feel.

Bottom / Pups in Cups
These cute cats and dogs peep out of a stack of cups that have mid-century-style pattern motifs.

Opposite / Feathers and Fluff
A set of six greetings cards featuring cute drawings of owls, bunnies, bears, and so on, designed by Amy Taylormade for a high street store. To create variety a mix of background designs are used, featuring either ruled lines or a grid.

Wishing you a HOPPY BIRTHDAY filled with Fun!

happy BIRTHDAY To You happy BIRTHDAY to You

Wishing you a BIRTHDAY With lots of Love

Special Wishes just for you With lots of Love on your BIRTHDAY

Have a Great Day Enjoy yourself!

Wishing you a Purr-Fect Birthday With lots of Love

Andrea Turk

www.cinnamonjoestudio.com
info@cinnamonjoestudio.com

o8 // Andrea Turk is an artist from the Cinnamon Joe Studio, based in Northern Ireland. Andrea gained a BA(Hons) in Fashion and Textiles at the University of Ulster in Belfast, as well as a Diploma in Industrial Studies. On completing her degree, Andrea achieved a certificate for Women Entrepreneurs in Business, which led her to relocate to London. After 12 years of a varied career in fashion design, design management, trend forecasting and consultancy work for many high street children's brands, Andrea set up the Cinnamon Joe Studio in 2002. The Studio specializes in fun graphics for all aspects of the children's market, including clothing, bedding, stationery, interiors, and novelty. She has a wide and varied client base across the globe, and is privileged to represent an amazing group of talented artists. Along with Cinnamon Joe Studio, Andrea continues to freelance, produce commissioned pieces, design for the Studio collection, and license her work. She lives in Cullybackey, Northern Ireland with her dog, two cats, and husband Paul.

Top / Fun at the Zoo
These zoo animals were hand-drawn and then scanned and tweaked to create a wonderfully unique pattern. Lots of white space and clever use of a double outline evoke the fun of a colouring book.

Bottom left /
Seaside Doggies
A piece of grey knitwear scanned to make a beard, and newspaper for a paper hat are some of the added features in this delightful design that combines nautical and dog themes.

Bottom right /
Cute Little Bears
This collection shows Andrea's skill at putting together a range of co-ordinating prints and placements. Green fake fur, chunky knitwear and fabrics were the inspiration to add dimension to her fuzzy little creatures.

Overleaf /
Bunny's and Owl's Day Out
Cute characters filled with little details such as ruled paper and handwriting stand out against a darker ground. Linear flowers add pattern without detracting from the main motifs.

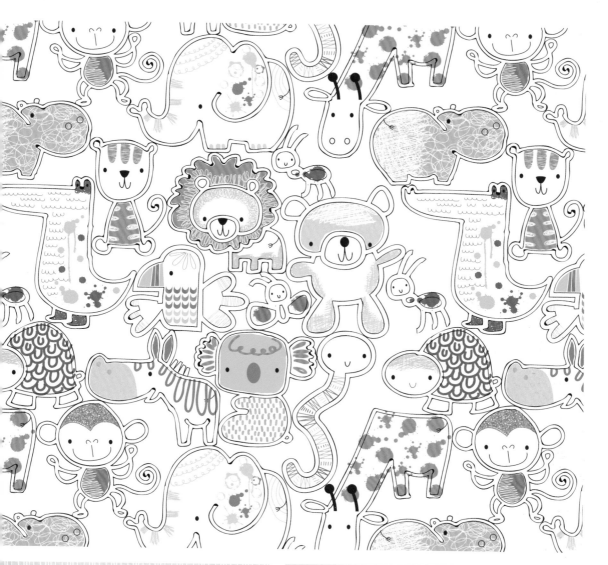

BiRtHdaY
BOY

B
sweeT E
CUTE A
playful R
HUGGaBLE

Angela Nickeas

www.hiccupstudiodesigns.blogspot.co.uk
www.pinklightdesign.com
hiccupstudiodesigns@yahoo.co.uk

09 // Angela Nickeas from Manchester in the UK studied for a BA (Hons) in Surface Pattern Design at Staffordshire University and set up Hiccup Studio Designs in 2010. Angela has over eight years' experience within the industry, mainly in the home textile and furnishing market, designing patterns and styling ranges for a number of major UK retailers and international clients. She also designs patterns for the scrapbooking, stationery, and giftware industry. Clients have included Oopsy Daisy, Robert Kaufman, Primark, Asda, Barnardo's, Macy's, Walmart, and Target. Her favourite motifs are bird and butterfly imagery, and her two young children are a constant source of joy and inspiration for her whimsical and quirky style.

Design Heroes: Lucienne Day, Tricia Guild (see pages 98–9), Carolyn Gavin (see pages 100–3)

Favourite Children's Illustrators: Russell Ayto, Leigh Hodgkinson, Sara Fanelli

Top / Happy Happy
Large, stylized blooms are surrounded by dynamic swirling lines and quirky motifs to give total coverage.

Bottom / Pop Floral
Floral design with a naive style where the flowers are anchored by loosely drawn grey lines to give it structure.

Opposite / Blooming Lovely
A whimsical pattern combining flowers and hand-drawn text, and demonstrating Angela's love of bird imagery. She also chose a favourite colour palette of pink, turquoise, olive, and grey.

LOVE HOPE JOY

THEO

Above / Theo
Personalized wall art of a birdie
'bursting with love, hope and joy'
and featuring fabulous typography
in a 'hand cut' style. Licensed to
Oopsy Daisy, Fine Art for Kids.

Opposite / Lola
This design originally started off as
a bespoke print for Angela's daughter's
bedroom wall. The playful bird in
a cheerful garden is intended to raise
a smile. Licensed to Oopsy Daisy,
Fine Art for Kids.

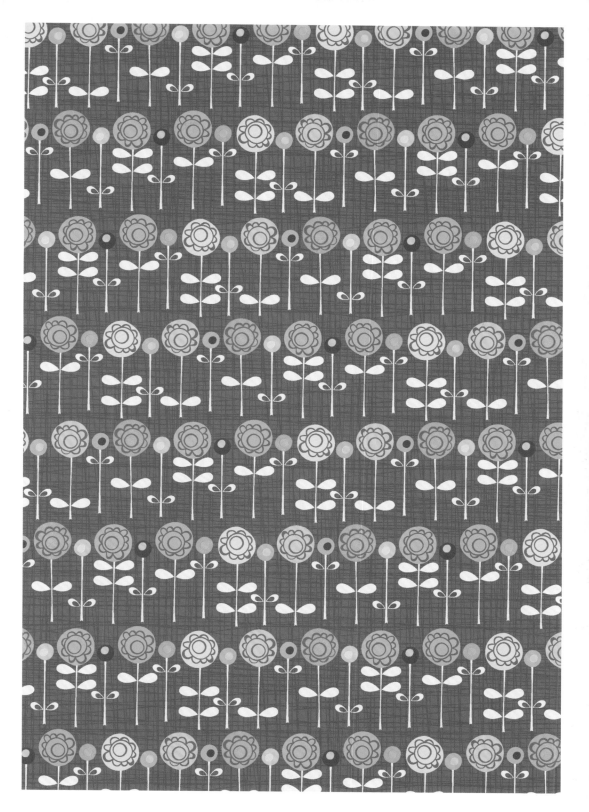

Opposite / Woodland Walk
A variety of cross hatching and texture adds depth and interest to this woodland scene where trees of varying scales and shapes fit together perfectly.

Above / Lollipop Floral
This pattern began life as a fun doodle and was recreated as a ditsy floral print in Photoshop. The round flowers in rows like lollipops evoke a simple, childlike drawing.

Ann Kelle

www.annkelle.com

10 // Kelle Boyd is from Tennessee and currently lives in Nashville. Kelle is a self-taught designer who studied a BA and MA in social work. Kelle designs under her studio label Ann Kelle Designs. In addition to her very successful textile designs, Kelle's work has been on the shelves of stationery boutiques and stores including Target, Barnes & Noble, QVC, and Walmart. Kelle also designs personalized stationery for Tiny Prints and Wedding Paper Divas. She is inspired by all the things we've always known and loved, from flying kites in the park to ice cream sundaes, to her favourite childhood Rainbow Brite doll – all the things she cherished as a child. Her dream commission would be to splatter her designs on the outside of an aeroplane, but for the immediate future Kelle would like to get more involved in children's home decor.

Design Hero: Orla Kiely
(see pages 232–3)

Favourite Children's Illustrators:
Shel Silverstein, Clement Hurd, Peter H. Reynolds

Top / Lollipop Love
Striped candy sugar lollipops look like spinning windmills in this bold design. The sticks give the layout a structure and its geometric nature makes it an ideal 'supportive' print to the more pictorial designs in the collection.

Bottom / Candy Toss
Inspiration for Kelle's collection came from her love of sweet foods. Sweets in wrappers create a geometric feel and the small scale of the sweets creates a good balance with larger motifs in the collection.

Opposite / I Dream of Sweets
A fabulous scattered or 'toss' pattern featuring colourful ice cream cones, iced lollies, and sweets. The gaps between the larger motifs are filled with circles and squares which resemble more tiny sweets.

Overleaf / Sundae Scoop
Scoops of ice cream made from stripes, spots, and checks sit in bowls that interlock together beautifully for a satisfying arrangement.

Audrey Jeanne

www.audreyjeanne.fr
ilovedrawing@orange.fr

11 // Audrey Jeanne is a French artist and illustrator based in Caen. She acquired a Master of Fine Arts degree at the University of Rennes, France. Audrey's work combines illustration and creating objects such as postcards, badges, fabric, and stationery. Audrey draws her inspiration from the 1950s and Asia, especially Japanese culture. She describes herself as an illustrator and designer of 'small, poetic objects'. Her work is stocked in shops all across the world from Mexico to Scotland and her clients have included ChaCha, L'Affiche Moderne and *Papier Mache* magazine. For a future ambition Audrey would love to design books, CD covers, make ceramics, and write a comic.

Design Hero: Picasso

Favourite Children's Illustrators: Kazue Takahashi, Juliette Binet, Kazuo Iwamura

Top & bottom /
ChaCha Stickers
Created as sheets of stickers for ChaCha – a stationery company based in Montpellier.

Opposite / ABC
A French alphabet poster. Audrey hopes her work and drawing style represent 'minimalism, symbolism, and humour'. Created for online art gallery L'Affiche Moderne. *www.laffichemoderne.com*

Opposite / Rodolphe
Designed for an A5 colouring
book illustrated throughout
by Audrey with line drawings
ready to be coloured. Edited
by ChaCha. Sold at
www.saison-boutique.com

Top / Kokeshi
Audrey's idea with this
beautiful Kokeshi illustration
on a postcard was to 'inject
a bit of purity and innocence
in this difficult world.'

Bottom left / Marinette
Design for a poster created
for ChaCha. Sold at
www.saison-boutique.com

Bottom right / Kitty and Bird
Designed for a poster
edited by OMM Design.
www.ommdesign.se

Aurélie Guillerey

www.flickr.com/photos/31447641@N05
aurelieguillerey@free.fr

12 // Aurélie Guillerey is an illustrator who lives in Rennes, France. She trained at the Ecole Nationale des Arts Décoratifs in Strasbourg, taking illustration classes in the workshop of Claude Lapointe. Aurélie finds inspiration for her work and style in posters from the 1950s and '60s and in the Moomin books and illustrations by Tove Jansson. Clients have included Gallimard, Casterman, Larousse, Très Tôt Théâtre and La Marelle Editions.

Favourite Children's Illustrators: Nathalie Parain, Roger Duvoisin, Sempé

Top / Mister Ballon
Created as a postcard for French publishers La Marelle Editions. A sweet little girl, a mischievous dog, and a whimsical balloon seller feature in this charming illustration, which is typical of Aurélie's work.

Bottom / Jour de Marché
Created as a postcard for French publishers La Marelle Editions. Aurélie uses a dry-brush technique to add small areas of spatter to her illustrations, evoking the classic illustrations of the '50s and '60s.

Opposite top / Bonsoir Porte Manteau!
Cover for a book which Aurélie wrote and illustrated for Parisian publisher JBZ & Cie. The title translates as 'Good evening coat stand!'. The image was created in Adobe Photoshop.

Opposite bottom / Garage
Created as a postcard for French publishers La Marelle Editions. Aurélie's mid-century influences are reflected clearly in her work, which has a timeless quality.

BONSOIR
PORTE MANTEAU !
AURÉLIE GUILLEREY

« Avec toi, j'irai jusqu'au bout du monde !... »

Above / Recipe Book
A recipe-themed notebook published by La Marelle Editions.
Aurélie used to work with traditional paint techniques
but later found she preferred the results of using a digital
graphics tablet and Adobe Photoshop.

Belle & Boo

www.belleandboo.com
www.belleandboo.blogspot.co.uk
mandy@belleandboo.com

13 // Belle & Boo is a company featuring the beautiful artwork of illustrator Mandy Sutcliffe. Mandy named the business after two of her favourite characters, Belle, a little girl, and Boo, her bunny rabbit companion. Mandy studied illustration at Leeds Metropolitan University, but her love for illustrating children truly blossomed whilst in Paris on a university exchange. She spent time drawing in the city's parks and found the Parisian children had such an elegant, old-fashioned charm about them. In 2007 Mandy set up Belle & Boo from her London flat, and in 2008 her good friend Kate joined her to organize the business part of her ever-growing children's lifestyle brand. Belle & Boo products now include greetings cards, gift wrap, art prints, clothes, cushions, tableware, fabrics, and stationery. The characters have also expanded into a series of storybooks published by Orchard, and a craft project book for adults with Quadrille Books. The future of Belle & Boo is very exciting with the launch of Baby Belle & Boo, a collaboration with a well-known British high street retailer, and the production of a Boo soft toy and a Belle doll. Who knows, Belle & Boo may even hop and skip onto our TV screens!

Design Heroes: Edouard Vuillard, Cath Kidston (see pages 72–7), Pierre Bonnard

Favourite Children's Illustrators: E.H. Shepard, Cicely Mary Barker, Mabel Lucie Attwell

54 / Print & Pattern

13 / Belle & Boo

Above / Belle & Boo Parade
There is a sense of the
familiar in Mandy's
illustrations which not only
appeals to children but also
has a nostalgic appeal to
adults. Here a parade of
children in brown outline
and muted flat colours
demonstrate Mandy's skill
at creating endearing and
timeless characters.

Opposite / Belle & Boo Invite
Belle has bobbed hair,
bright eyes, and wears cute
vintage clothing. She was
based in part on Mandy as
a child. Nostalgic in style
and concept, the colours
for Belle & Boo are generally
muted, but as this invite
needs to represent the fun
of a party Mandy has added
colour in the typography.

Left / Patience Brown
Paris and fashion have both
played a part in creating
the Belle & Boo aesthetic.
Mandy found the children of
Paris had very classic clothes
and hairstyles, and Mandy
now often looks to vintage
clothing for her inspiration.

Top left / I Baked This for You
Created as a Mother's Day
card. A little girl has baked
a cake and is accompanied by
typography that uses a mixture
of handwritten script and ornate,
decorative capitals.

Top right /
I Grew These for You
Created as a Mother's Day card.
By not using white backgrounds
Mandy has instantly created a
vintage look with this little boy
and his daffodils.

Bottom / Boo Cushion
Boo is Belle's adorable bunny
rabbit companion and confidant.
This cushion features a hand-
embroidered Boo motif on the
front and a screen-printed Boo
motif in repeat on the back.

Opposite / I Like Your Bow
This design features a wonderfully
muted colour palette and a dress
that will appeal to any little girl.
The addition of a charming pull-
along elephant toy adds a sense
of imagination and play.

biroRobot

www.biroRobot.co.uk
www.biroRobot.bigcartel.com
studio@birorobot.co.uk

14 // biroRobot is a design studio producing bespoke illustrations and hand-pulled, limited edition prints. The studio is a collaboration between sisters and independently successful illustrators, Lisa and Elena Gomez. Between them they bring over 25 years' illustration and design experience to biroRobot. Their past work has included illustrating children's books, surface pattern design, editorial, cards, calendars, ceramics, apparel and art prints. Combined clients include Habitat, Ikea, Paperchase, Sainsbury's, BBC, *Homes & Gardens* magazine and Waterstones.

Design Heroes: Alexander Girard, Saul Bass, Charley Harper

Favourite Children's Illustrators:
Lisa – Alain Grée (see pages 10–15)
Elena – Květa Pacovská

Top / Ruff
Hand-drawn, coloured and finished in Adobe Illustrator. Cute dogs are rendered using straight, angular lines and placed on a background grid of lines. From the biroRobot surface pattern design portfolio.

Bottom / Kawaii Dino
These dinosaurs have been given the aesthetic cuteness of Japanese Kawaii, making them friendly and appealing to children. Created in Illustrator, from the biroRobot surface pattern design collection.

'Stacking Buses'   1/35   biroRobot 2011

Blanca Gómez

cosasminimas.com
www.etsy.com/shop/blancucha

15 // Blanca Gómez is an illustrator from Madrid, Spain. She studied Publicity at university in Madrid and in Milan, but soon realized that publicity was not for her and enrolled in evening classes at a design school. Blanca says she is a nostalgic person and things from the past are very inspirational to her. 'Mid-century designers were super heroes,' she says. Her client list includes Chronicle Books, Dwell, Monocle, *Creative Review, The Daily Telegraph,* The Land of Nod, *O* magazine and card publisher Lagom, for whom most of these designs were created. Blanca's website is named Cosa Minimas, which translates to mean 'tiny things'.

Design Hero: Alexander Girard

Favourite Children's Illustrator: Sempé

Above /
In the Neighbourhood
A digital illustration created as a print for Blanca's Etsy shop. A little girl holds a string of transparent overlapping balloons.

Opposite top left /
Big Cake Greeting Card
Opposite top right /
Rain Girl Greeting Card
Opposite bottom left /
Bird Girl Greeting Card
Opposite bottom right /
Flower Girl Greeting Card
All created for the Poco Collection of greetings cards published by Lagom. The designs have a retro feel with their mid-century inspired characters, but still look fresh in style thanks to Blanca's clean lines, pattern fills, and modern colour palette.

Boden

www.boden.co.uk

16 // Boden began life as a menswear business when it was founded in 1991 by Johnnie Boden. It soon expanded into womenswear, and its childrenswear label Mini Boden followed in 1996. Their style is fun and quirky, although the emphasis is definitely on high quality and durability rather than on disposable trends. Collections produced seasonally for boys and girls usually contain colourful stripes, cute placement motifs (that often have extra details such as appliqué) and colourful prints for use on everything from shorts to pyjamas. In 2007 the company further expanded when their Baby Boden range was launched.

Top / Baby Cowboy Tee
Called 'When I Grow Up', this cowboy came from a range of Baby Tees. The design is made from appliqué.

Middle / Boys' Plane Tee
A front view of a jumbo jet has been boldly appliquéd on a float background. From a collection of boys' tees based on 'Vehicles' which also featured a motorcycle and train design.

Bottom / Baby Duck Tee
A pretty little t-shirt for baby girls featuring a duck motif made from appliqué. Edged stitching at the neckline gives it an extra Baby Boden touch.

Top / Whales
A colourful design for boys' beachwear, shorts, etc. that cleverly shows the whale motifs rippled and distorted as if they were underwater.

Bottom / Seagulls
Perfect for the seaside, these simply rendered seagulls have a nautical feel and are designed for boys or girls.

Opposite / Skate Dogs
A quirky print featuring skateboarding dogs gives this boys'
print a cool edge and a sense of humour.

Above / Doggies
Little puppies in grey and white are scattered across this
repeat pattern design. A modern twist is provided by the
bright pink and lime green collars.

Bumpkin

www.bumpkinbears.com
www.bumpkin.etsy.com
catherine@bumpkinbears.com

17 // Catherine Young is originally from the UK but now lives in a small rural village in Belgium near the artistic city of Antwerp. Catherine has studied Art and Textile Design, Communication and Image Studies, and Interior and Garden Design. She named her design business Bumpkin after the nickname her Granny gave her: 'Country Bumpkin'. She began by creating collectors' bears but then expanded into a range of illustrated prints and paper goods. Catherine is influenced by the English traditions and values she was raised with. She loves cottage gardens, wildlife, handmade pottery, the children's books she grew up with, and vintage embroidery. Catherine is represented by Teresa Kietlinski of the TK Prospect Literary Agency in New York for writing and illustrating children's books and is open to any licensing queries. Looking into the future, Catherine would love to design wallpaper, textiles, and childrenswear. She also plans to extend the reach of her wall art, stationery, and party goods by adding more stockists.

Design Heroes: William Morris, Angie Lewin, Anna Maria Horner

Favourite Children's Illustrators: Beatrix Potter, E.H. Shepard, Mandy Sutcliffe

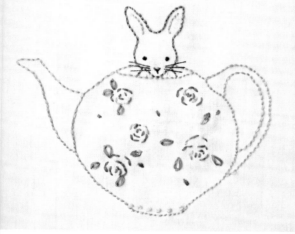

Opposite top /
Bunny and her Teacup
Part of Catherine's 'Friends
for Tea' range, inspired
by the English tradition
of afternoon tea. Created
for wall art, badges, cards
and party goods such
as cupcake toppers and
invitations. An adorable
bunny sits on top of a stack
of vintage teacups, which
were hand drawn in pencil
and then painted digitally
in Photoshop.

Opposite bottom /
A Lamb Called Buttercup
A delicate sketch of a cute
lamb in the spring flowers
inspired by days on a farm
as a child. Hand drawn and
then digitally painted, it
was created for wall art and
stationery in her Etsy Shop.

Top left /
Sweet Dreams Embroidery
An illustration of a super-
sweet mouse tucked in
a patchwork quilt was
recreated as a stitching
pattern so customers
can easily replicate the
embroidery themselves on
cushions, quilts, clothing, etc.

Middle /
Bunny and her Teapot
Catherine loves handmade
pottery and vintage china
and incorporates them into
her work. These delicately
embroidered roses were
inspired by an old teapot.
She adores country living
and the homespun cottage
style. Created for a pattern
sold online at Etsy.

Bottom /
Tea Time in the Snow
A bunny uses a teacup
as a sledge in Catherine's
hand-stitched artwork.
In this busy, high-tech
world Catherine is inspired
to create illustrations that
are both comforting and
magical, and where nature
and family are cherished.

Above /
Bunny and her Cupcakes
An embroidery stitched
using Catherine's illustrations
and created as a pattern
for customers who then
stitch them as part of quilts,
cushions, clothing and wall art.
Sold online in her Etsy Shop.

Buttongirl Designs

www.buttongirl.co.uk
trudy@buttongirl.co.uk

18 // Trudy Willoughby of Buttongirl Designs is based in Bedfordshire, UK. Trudy studied at the Loughborough School of Art and Design and after graduation freelanced for a number of London textile design studios designing women's prints and embroideries for the European and American markets. 'This period was so valuable as I learnt so much about the world of surface pattern design,' recalls Trudy. It inspired her to develop and create a small greetings card company, Buttongirl Designs. All her designs are hand-stitched and appliquéd in her studio, which is a treasure trove full of sparkly things, patterned ribbons, quirky buttons, and rows of colourful fabric. Trudy finds inspiration in day-to-day life, her nephews, and her love of colour, pattern, texture, and embellishment. She also freelances for the childrenswear market designing appliqués and embroideries. One day Trudy would love to have her own children's range under the label Buttongirl Designs.

Design Heroes: Jane Ormes, Dottie Angel, Lisa Congdon

Favourite Children's Illustrators: Jane Hissey, Oliver Jeffers, Alice and Martin Provensen

All / 'Off to the Zoo' Greetings Card Range
A range of children's age greetings cards based on quirky zoo animal illustrations. All designs are hand-stitched, appliquéd, and lovingly embellished with unique buttons, ribbons, pom poms, and trinkets bought from markets, charity shops, and haberdasheries. Trudy says, 'I'm definitely into the eclectic look and nothing must match.'

2 today

love

3 today

Hello

...day

5 today

Love

Castle

www.castleandthings.com.au
hello@castleandthings.com.au

19 //   Rachel Castle founded her business, Castle, in 2008 after she had made a small range of bedlinen for friends and family. It proved such a hit she decided to turn it into a commercial venture. Rachel studied Communications at RMIT in Melbourne, Australia, and has since worked in the design industry for 20 years, including a spell at The Conran Shop and co-founding her own agency, The Nest, in London. Rachel now lives in Northbridge, a suburb of Sydney, Australia. From here she works both as a freelance writer and stylist for Australian lifestyle magazines, and runs Castle, designing and selling bedlinen, cushions, and artworks. All of Castle's handmade artworks are either screen-printed or sewn by Rachel and her mother Jillian Patching.

Design Heroes: David Band, Jonathan Adler

Favourite Children's Illustrator: Paul Rand

Above / Raindrop
Beautiful coloured raindrops including fluoro yellow and neon pink fall from a light blue cloud in this fun design. Made from felt and acrylic hand-stitched onto vintage linen.

Right / I Love Homework
Rachel is well known for her typographic embroideries, which often spell out sentimental messages or song lyrics. Here she has created a humorous artwork for a child's room. Made from felt and linen on a linen base.

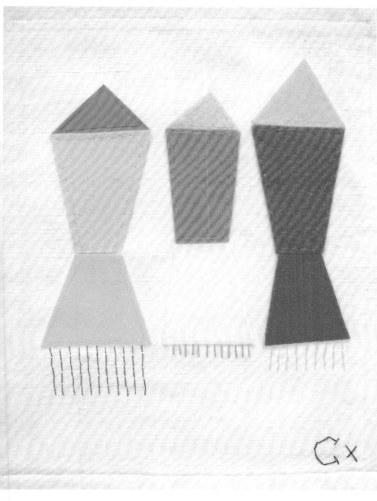

Top / 3 Rockets
Using simple cut-out pieces of felt and acrylic with bright neon colours, Rachel has distilled the images of the rockets down to their simplest shapes, and yet they are instantly recognizable. Hand-stitched embroidery on vintage linen.

Bottom left / Little Rainbow
This design would make a real splash of colour in any room. Made from felt and linen, the bold colours of this abstracted rainbow are set against a darker base of Belgian flax linen for extra pop.

Bottom right / Patch Circle Big
These tiny pieces of felt, linen, and wool have been hand-stitched in a circle on linen fabric to create a bright and cheery design. Many of Rachel's artworks are one-of-a-kind, but a good selection is always available and she takes on commissions.

Cath Kidston

www.cathkidston.co.uk

20 // Cath Kidston opened her first shop in London in 1993, selling vintage fabrics and brightly painted junk furniture. She grew up in Redenham, Hampshire, and fondly remembered the style and decor of her childhood country home. Her clever reworking of the British country house style, which she gave a fresh and colourful modern edge, soon made her business a huge success. Her patterns have been hugely influential and are instantly recognizable, especially her floral rose prints. Her main influence is vintage fabric, where she will take the essence of a design and reinvent it with a contemporary twist. Cath and her design team will often visit antiques fairs in search of their inspiration. Now a global lifestyle brand, Cath Kidston's nostalgic designs are perfectly suited to children. In 2008 she launched her 'Cath Kids' label with fabulous prints on clothing, toys, nursery decor, stationery, tableware, bags, and more.

Above / Scrap Book
Capturing a bygone era, this children's 'Baby Zoo' scrapbook shows perfectly how traditional design can appeal to the contemporary market.

Opposite top / Circus
This vintage-inspired print offers a classic, timeless look for any nursery. The soft and delicate palette of colours captures all the fun of the circus with clowns, elephants, lions, and acrobats. With scenes like a dog riding a bicycle with a cat on his head who is balancing two mice, children cannot fail to be captivated. Cath Kidston produced this design on wallpaper and fabric.

Opposite bottom left / Painting Set
Recalling products of yesteryear, this traditional tin set of paints and brushes features a circus elephant.

Opposite bottom right / Guards Suitcase
This quirky guards design was created in 2012, the year of the Queen's Diamond Jubilee and the London Olympics, when London-themed imagery became enormously popular. Cath Kidston came up with a classic design featuring regimented rows of stylized guardsmen in traditional red, white, and blue. Shown here on a children's suitcase that is just the right size for summer trips and weekends away.

Overleaf / Cowboy
This cowboy print is a classic Cath Kidston children's design that has become synonymous with the brand. Instantly recognizable, it features retro cowboy heroes in action with horses, wagons, cacti, and ranches. Available as wallpaper, fabric, and a whole range of children's products such as bedlinen, melamine tableware, and bath towels.

Above / Dinosaurs
This fun, retro-inspired print features colourful dinosaurs in a land of volcanoes and exotic trees. Perfect for little boys, it was produced on, amongst other things, bedding and pyjamas, ensuring bedtime would never be boring.

Opposite / Vintage Cars
A fabulous pattern for boys of all ages, this design captures the excitement of the early days of motor racing. Available on wallpaper and fabric, it was inspired by old vintage Formula One annuals.

Charlotte Swiden

swiden.com.au
info@swiden.com.au

21 //   Charlotte Swiden grew up in Malmö on the southern shores of Sweden, but since 2005 has lived Melbourne, Australia. Charlotte studied Graphic Design in Sweden and Argentina, and Communication Design in Melbourne. She worked as a Senior Designer at Swedish stationery company kikki.K for three years before starting her own business, Swiden, creating tablewares. Charlotte also freelances as a graphic designer on the side for a wide variety of clients, creating anything from promotional material to animation props and puppets. Her designs and illustrations are mostly influenced by her Swedish heritage and love of nature, both in style and story. 'I think it's just something that happens, the objects and way of life that surrounded me growing up come through in my style and the way I work,' she says. Going forward, Charlotte dreams of spending more time designing and would like to hand some of the production chores over to someone else. She has folders full of ideas and sketches that she would love to work on and wants to explore more new materials and work with porcelain, timber, and fabric.

Design Heroes: Karin Larsson, David Band, Signe Persson-Melin

Favourite Children's Illustrators: Tove Jansson, Stig Lindberg, Charley Harper

Top / Ice Cream Tray
Charlotte has pared this illustration of an ice cream down to its simplest forms. It was hand-drawn and then digitally retouched. Here it is featured on a Scandinavian birch tray produced in Sweden. As Charlotte says, 'I design things I need and would like to have in my own home.'

Bottom /
Tivolivat Cushion Cover: Ferris
A fantastic abstract representation of Ferris wheels becomes a bold geometric print, shown here on a cushion that was designed and individually sewn at Swiden and printed in Australia using water-based non-toxic dyes.

Top left /
Tivolivat Poster: Ferris Wheels
Inspired by fun park rides, fairy floss, and Ferris wheels. The hand-drawn sketches and multicoloured tape compositions on this wall art print were developed and finished digitally. The Ferris wheels are arranged in rows with each one containing a variety of shapes in bold colours.

Top right /
Tivolivat Poster: Round
The wheels are randomly dispersed across the print to form a dynamic geometric poster. The Tivolivat collection gets its name from a play on words in Swedish. Tivoli, another word for fun park, and Livat, meaning exhilarating or lively. Printed on uncoated matt paper.

Bottom /
Tivolivat Wooden Decorations
Perfect for stylish and cheerful nursery ornaments, these Ferris wheels are made from birch ply treated with linseed oil. Making things that have a beautiful, tactile feeling is as important to Charlotte as applying the right graphics. A limited edition designed and produced in Australia.

Claire Louise Milne

www.clairelouisemilne.com
www.needlebook.ca
claire@clairelouisemilne.com

22 // Claire Louise Milne is based in Toronto, Ontario, Canada. She studied Graphic Design and Illustration at George Brown College and Children's Book Illustration at the Ontario College of Art & Design. Her clients have included Scholastic, Bebop Books, Happy House, McGraw-Hill and The Royal Ontario Museum. Claire's work is inspired and informed by vintage children's book illustration, especially the fairy tales and storybooks she grew up with. She also loves vintage fabrics, particularly 1930s feedsack prints, and the natural forms of plants, flowers, and trees. The beautiful films of Miyazaki, such as *Spirited Away*, have also been a recent source of inspiration. Her dream design commission would be to illustrate a new edition of *The Best-Loved Doll* by Rebecca Caudill.

Design Heroes: Heather Ross, Lotta Jansdotter, Cath Kidston (see pages 72–7)

Favourite Children's Illustrators: Marc Boutavant (see pages 196–9), Tiphanie Beeke, Adrienne Adams

Kitten climbing

Top / Kitten Climbing
Cloth picture books for babies have been a long tradition in children's design. Claire created a 12-page book that would fit onto just one fat quarter of fabric to sell in her Needlebook Spoonflower shop. Kitten climbing is just one of the beautiful pages.

Bottom / Kite Friends
The strings of these kites create a diagonal stripe on which to anchor the super-sweet characters. Created for a fabric print on the textile website Spoonflower.com

Opposite / Paris Poodle
This two-colour fabric design, created for Spoonflower, has more of a vintage feel. The poodles on bicycles are animated by the dotty background.

Creepy Tree

www.creepytree.co.uk
www.tinamuat.com
hello@creepytree.co.uk

23 // Tina Muat is based in Brighton in the UK. She has a degree in Graphic Design, specializing in Illustration, although Tina feels she learnt everything she needed from art galleries and books. Tina began creating her own screen-printed cards and selling them to small boutiques. This encouraged her to launch 'Creepy Tree Designs' in 2011, designing and publishing greetings cards and wrapping paper. Her work is influenced by her observations of everyday occurrences, where she looks for the humour in a situation and how it may be changed or taken out of context. Tina loves the weird and wonderful world of Dr. Seuss and is drawn to sarcastic humour and the silly, sinister, and surreal. Her ambition would be to design for the children's magazine *Anorak* and create more Creepy Tree Designs.

Design Heroes: Kenneth Townsend, Saul Bass, Edie Harper

Favourite Children's Illustrators: Miroslav Sasek, Dick Bruna, Dr. Seuss

Top / Jolly Good Fello
Tina has pared this tree down to its geometric essence and filled it with sweetly stylized and colourful birds. The lively typography is typical of Tina's illustration style.

Bottom / Bundle of Joy
Tina cleverly worked the hand-drawn type and motifs on this new baby greetings card into the shape of a baby's mobile.

Opposite top /
Juggler & Elephant
Elephants and circus characters are a popular theme for children's design and these two card designs both have plenty of movement and colour.

Opposite bottom /
Cowboy & Native Girl
Tina's work exudes colour and joy, and children can easily identify with her bright colours and cartoon-like forms.

party
time

howdy

how!

Dan Stiles

www.danstiles.com
dan@danstiles.com

₂₄ // Dan Stiles is based in Portland, Oregon, in the US, where he is best known for his rock posters for bands like the Arctic Monkeys and Sonic Youth. But more recently Dan turned his hand to designing for children with several collections for Birch Fabrics. Collections like 'Marine', 'Mod Squad', and 'Next Stop' gave Dan the chance to experiment with colour and pattern. Dan finds his influences come from a variety of sources including classic skateboard graphics, album covers, modern art, Japanese design, old comic books, and vintage packaging. He also loves commercial illustrations from the 1950s and '60s, many of which are anonymous. Dan's past clients have included Nike, Gap and MTV.

Design Heroes: Paul Rand, Saul Bass, Alexander Girard, James Flora

Favourite Children's Illustrators: Mary Blair, Miroslav Sasek

Top / Owl
Here Dan has managed to make an owl full of character using only geometric shapes. Originally created as a screen-printed art print for his solo art show and later licensed for various children's products.

Bottom / Birdhouses
Dan often uses elements of pattern within his illustration work, such as the use of quatrefoil motifs here. The use of light and dark colours also gives great depth to the bird houses. Screen-printed art print created as part of a series for his solo show at Tilde.

Opposite / Birdland
This fun bird print demonstrates how Dan is inspired by simple shapes and repeats. All the birds appear to have been made by cutting away portions of a circle. A self-initiated design that is part of a series of bird-related patterns created for licensing.

Above / Whale Love
One of the prints from Dan's nautical-themed 'Marine' fabric collection for Birch. The stylized waves made of semicircles show his love of simplicity and the purity of form.

Opposite top / Friends of Trees
Bold triangle shapes with interesting opacity effects make for a very colourful and friendly design, possibly inspired by Dan's days of working as a screen-printer where overprinting was a big part of the process (i.e. printing one ink on top of another to create a third colour). Originally created as the CD cover for a folk music compilation.

Bottom / Part of Dan's series of Sellwood prints, created for an art show in Portland. Screen-printed art print created as part of a series.

Bottom right / Dan uses flat shapes to create each creature. He says of his own creations, 'I don't draw a picture and then colour it in. The colours and their shapes are the picture.' Screen-printed art print for his solo show and afterwards licensed for various children's products.

Dawn Bishop

dawndraws.blogspot.co.uk
dawneloise@hotmail.com

25 // Dawn Bishop is based in London. She studied for a BA (Hons) in Illustration at Loughborough University and now works as a designer specializing in children's print/graphics and stationery. Dawn has amassed an impressive client list but just some of those she has created for include Mothercare, Primark, Boots, Target, Gap, and Zutano. She finds inspiration in pattern and colour, and loves animals and the countryside. Dawn's dream commission would be to illustrate a children's book one day.

Design Heroes: Tim Walker, Charley Harper, Miroslav Sasek

Favourite Children's Illustrators: Lauren Child, Quentin Blake, Brian Wildsmith

Top /
Butterflies and Flowers
Delicate little butterflies are a perfect motif for girls as they can be dainty yet graphic and colourful. Initially hand-drawn then edited in Adobe Illustrator for baby/toddler girls. Sold to Galison.

Bottom / Sleeping Beauty
This print has a nighttime theme with Sleeping Beauty, her cute teddy bear, the moon, and a sleeping owl. Perfect for baby/toddler girls' nightwear or bedlinen. Initially hand-drawn then taken into Photoshop. Sold to Turner Bianca.

Opposite / Boys' Toys
This charming and sketchy boys' print was initially hand-drawn then taken into Photoshop and worked up for use on baby/toddler boys' clothing. Sold to Pumpkin Patch.

Opposite / Sweets in Jars
In this beautiful design the jars are drawn in delicate black linework whilst the contents are solid blocks of candy colours. Hand-drawn then taken into Illustrator. Sold to GAP.

Above / Ice-cream Vans
This fun summer print featuring colourful ice-cream vans is perfect for evoking all the happiness of a holiday or trip to the seaside. Hand-drawn and worked up in Adobe Illustrator for toddler girls. Sold to Marks & Spencer.

Dawn Machell

www.pop-i-cok.blogspot.com
dawn@dawnmachell.com
rep: www.mysugarcube.com

26 // Dawn Machell is a freelance designer based in West Yorkshire, England. Dawn studied Fashion Design in Salford and began her career by making children's clothes for her own label before joining a company where she learnt all the skills needed to be a childrenswear designer. She later worked for Mamas & Papas, designing graphics for clothing and nursery ranges. It was after having children of her own that Dawn decided to work as a freelance designer for a better-quality family life. Dawn is inspired by children's books and would love to write and illustrate her own one day, or perhaps produce a trend book based on a kids print theme. She also enjoys Pinterest and lots of shopping to keep her creative juices flowing. Clients have included Pumpkin Patch, Primark, Next, BHS, Disney, and of course Mamas & Papas. One day she would love to design for Oilily. In 2011 Dawn took part in the Sketchbook Project with her work, *It's Raining Dogs and Cats.* The project involved sending out blank sketchbooks to artists for them to fill in and return.

Design Heroes:
Jillian Phillips (see pages 156-9),
Orla Kiely (see pages 232-3),
Helen Dardik (see pages 128-31)

Favourite Children's Illustrators:
Chris Haughton, Lauren Child,
Leigh Hodgkinson

Top / Not Raining Dogs and Cats
Dawn's typography is always unique and interesting. Here she has used a mixture of hand-drawn fonts from scribble to shadow and hand-cut, which fit perfectly with the charming characters.

Bottom / Not a Dog or a Cat
After illustrating lots of cats and dogs for her sketchbook, Dawn felt the urge to work on something different. Dawn uses a naive shape filled with pattern and this is all that is needed to create a rabbit.

Top / Rain Has Gone / Take Me For a Walk
Two more pages from the *It's Raining Dogs and Cats* sketchbook. Different sizes of grid balance each other beautifully beneath the illustrations and the pages have been carefully co-ordinated.

Bottom left / Raining Dogs and Cats
This was the title page of Dawn's sketchbook. All the books issued as part of the project were the same but Dawn cut an aperture in the kraft card cover to reveal this little dog illustration.

Bottom right / 100
A cute mouse character was used to celebrate the fact that Dawn had now written 100 posts on her pop-i-cock blog. She uses pattern fills to great effect; here only the balloon and mouse's ear hole are left unfilled so the illustration is packed with interest.

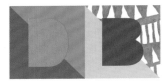

Dennis Bennett

www.dennisbennett.net
badgershirts.spreadshirt.de
post@dennisbennett.net

27 // Dennis Bennett is based in Frankfurt am Main, Germany. Dennis actually studied Medicine and is a qualified physician working in psychiatry but he also loves to design and illustrate. He has illustrated several book covers for a German publisher. In 2010 Dennis was also the winner of the Boba/Spoonflower Design Contest. His nature themed 'Tweet' design was used on Boba Baby Carriers and has been the most popular design in their collection. He hopes to get more involved in design whilst still working as a doctor. Dennis takes his influence from modern art and especially loves the mid-century modern 1950s aesthetic. His inspiration comes from his childhood memories, cartoon classics, and Japanese art and anime.

Design Heroes: Charley Harper, Mary Blair, Alexander Girard

Favourite Children's Illustrators: Maurice Sendak

Right /
Springtime in the Forest
This forest scene features not only the typical woodland creatures you'd expect to find but also lots of ornate and decorative patterns within the trees.

Right / Day in the Jungle
Dennis is known as
Dennis the Badger on the
Spoonflower website.
This design, featuring highly
stylized animals hiding within
architectural plants, was
another competition winner
in their 'Palette-restricted
botanical print contest'.

Designers Guild Kids

www.designersguild.com
info@designersguild.com

28 // Designers Guild was founded in 1970 by Tricia Guild and the company has gone on to become one of Britain's leading luxury home and lifestyle companies. The company designs and wholesales furnishing fabrics, wall coverings, upholstery, accessories, and bed and bath collections worldwide. Designers Guild have won many awards for both design and business achievements. It was in the 1980s that they launched their first collection specifically for children. The collection, which was called 'Merry Go Round', was a collection of prints and co-ordinating wallpapers.
Now Designers Guild's Kids label produces a new collection every two to three years, as well as specially designed bed and bath accessories every season, with all designs being created in-house in their own studio, which is headed by Tricia Guild. Based in London, they have a flagship store and homestore on the Kings Road, and a second homestore on Marylebone High Street. The Designers Guild brand is now represented globally.

Top / All Around the World
This beautiful pattern cleverly manages to be both fun and educational. Colourful motifs stand out on the white land set in a sea of sketchy waves.

Bottom left / Daisy Patch
A design for girls of all ages, this print has its roots in traditional patchwork but is updated with lively floral drawings and fresh pastel colours.

Bottom right / My Best Friend
A modern, colourful print featuring hand-painted animal friends and fashionable motifs on a graph paper patterned background. There is a superb contrast between the loosely rendered motifs and the tight, straight lines of the background.

Ecojot

www.ecojot.com
www.designerjots.squarespace.com
info@ecojot.com

29 // Ecojot was formed in 2007 and is based in Toronto, Ontario, Canada. They specialize in creating eco-friendly stationery products that feature colourful and inspirational designs. Featuring the fabulous design work of Ecojot co-founder Carolyn Gavin, Ecojot produce a wide range of notebooks, sketchbooks, and jotters for children, as well as baby books, albums, and nursery prints. Ecojot also design for clients such as Paperchase and Pottery Barn Kids. Carolyn finds inspiration for her designs from animals, the environment, and nature. She also loves anything to do with flowers, bright colours, and exotic patterns. Ecojot exhibits regularly at trade shows in New York and are stocked at more than 1,000 locations around the world, including Barnes & Noble and Indigo Books. 'I adore designing for the young market, especially kids,' Carolyn says. 'The audience allows one to be a little freer with colour, expression, and whimsy. It's such fun and there really aren't too many restrictions, which shows in a most wonderful way in the work.' All Ecojot's paper and board is 100 per cent post-consumer recycled. They only use acid- and chlorine-free paper and print with vegetable-based inks. They are also committed to a program called 'Give' where they give free books to children who are in need.

Design Heroes: Charley Harper, Nate Williams, Helen Dardik (see pages 128–31)

Favourite Children's Illustrators: Brian Wildsmith, Roger Duvoisin, Margaret Bloy Graham

Top / Mama Bird Breen Baby Book
A bird and her baby are rendered in gorgeous pastel colours on this Ecojot keepsake to record your baby's first year with milestones, firsts and favourites.

Bottom / Baby Animals Wrap
All the motifs and characters from Carolyn's baby designs come together on this sheet of recycled wrapping paper. The colourful elephants, birds, and giraffes are lifted by a neutral coloured dotty background.

Top / Dog Fishing
A party invitation is given
a nautical feel but dogs
are the fishermen, not
people, to add that extra
charm. The background
and boat feature images
of woodgrain.

Bottom / Jellyfish
Smiling jellyfish make an
unusual subject matter
for this kids' birthday party
invitation. But Carolyn's
beautiful colour palette
and friendly faces turn
them into cute companions.

Right / Growing Houses
Growth Chart
Designed to record a little
one's growth, this chart
is packed with colour and
interesting textures. The
wooden houses stand out
on the dot-filled background,
ensuring children will look
forward to seeing what lives
inside each house as they
get taller.

Opposite / Animals Sketchbook
Cute and colourful critters such as bears, foxes, cats, dogs, and owls really brighten up this cover design for a sketchbook. The Ecojot message is that they all live peacefully together.

Above / Sweet Cupcakes Sketchbook
Happy cupcakes in a variety of stripes and designs sit side by side on this cover design for a kids' sketchbook. With so many designs to view, young artistic imaginations can really be engaged.

Ed Emberley

www.embrgroupinc.com
www.cloud9fabrics.com

30 // Ed Emberley was born in 1931 in Massachusetts. He attended the Massachusetts College of Art in Boston, where he met his wife, Barbara, who was studying fashion design. He later completed his training at the Rhode Island School of Design. Ed began his working career in advertising but quickly turned to illustrating children's books. Ed is most famous for his 1970s instructional drawing books that showed readers anyone can draw by using simple techniques, and these very popular titles are still in print today. Ed's daughter Rebecca is the Emberley family's brand/business manager and looks after his licensing through their company EMBR. She created their style guide and makes sure licensees keep within the brand's sensibilities. Rebecca worked closely with Cloud9 Fabrics to create the 'Happy Drawing' fabric collection. Ed loved the green aspect of Cloud9 who use only 100 per cent certified organic cotton. They are based in Cranford, New Jersey, and were founded by Michelle Engel Bencsko and Gina Pantastico. Michelle put together the fabric repeat designs to bring Ed Emberley's wonderful drawings to a whole new market.

Design Heroes: Peter Max, Charles and Ray Eames, Marimekko (see pages 204-7)

Favourite Children's Illustrators: Mary Blair, Charley Harper, Alice and Martin Provensen

Left / Alligators
The 'Happy Drawing' collection is based on some of the iconic images from Ed Emberley's first how-to-draw book, *Ed Emberley's Drawing Book of Animals*, originally published in 1970. Stylized alligators with strong lines look great in bright green set over dark charcoal grey.

Above / Elephants
A herd of elephants in shades of grey are mixed with other more colourful Ed Emberley motifs. This design clearly shows Ed's theory that by using basic shapes such as circles, semi-circles and triangles you can draw anything.

Overleaf / Frogs
This repeat is tightly filled with fun, stylized frogs, but manages to keep a light and airy feel thanks to the heavy use of white.

Opposite / Lions and Tigers
The sketchy strokes of the lions' manes are interspersed
with the contrasting stronger lines of the tigers to give a
print with maximum overall coverage.

Above / Forest Friends
This print brings together many of Ed's iconic characters
from his drawing books in one bold print. In keeping with
the animals, the colour palette is natural and earthy.

Elissa Hudson

www.elissahudson.com
www.elissahudson.etsy.com
elissahudson@gmail.com

31 // Elissa Hudson is based in Leawood, Kansas, and studied first a BA at the University of Kansas followed by an MFA at Savannah College of Art and Design. Elissa especially loves illustration and hand lettering; nothing makes her happier than knowing that her artwork made someone smile. Her clients have included *Cricket* Magazine and *Cross Stitcher* Magazine. Elissa is influenced by children's books, fashion, interior design, and anything that is happy or that sparkles. For the future, Elissa will continue striving to expand her styling in illustration and lettering and would welcome any opportunities that may come as a result.

Design Heroes: Kate Spade, Sabrina Ward Harrison, Allan Drummond

Favourite Children's Illustrator: Lauren Child

Left / Colourful Alphabet
Elissa's love of hand-drawn
lettering is evident in this
alphabet print created for
her Etsy shop. 'I had a lot of
fun playing with the different
stylings of the letters,' she
says. Once again the framed
border focuses the eye into
the middle.

Above / A is for Apple
A deceptively simple print
that has a retro schoolroom
feel to it. The yellow frame
draws the eye straight
towards the bright blue
three-dimensional letter
'A'. It was hand-drawn and
scanned for finishing in
Photoshop.

Ellen Crimi-Trent

www.ellencrimitrent.com
ellencrimitrent.typepad.com
crimitrent@earthlink.net

32 // Ellen Crimi-Trent currently lives in Abington, Massachusetts. She studied Illustration at Pratt Institute in Brooklyn, New York. Ellen went to college originally to become a fashion designer but changed her major to Illustration because she wanted to become a children's book illustrator. Her dream came true in 2012 when her Schoolies book line was published by Priddy Books. Ellen licenses her designs for use on a variety of products but would love to create a bedding collection. Her previous clients have included JCPenney, Target, Enesco, and Clothworks. Ellen's sons have always influenced her design work. She ends up making illustrations around whatever the boys seem to be into at the time, like dinosaurs, trains, trucks, animals, and even crazy characters. 'I show them what I am working on to get feedback,' she says. 'I am always interested in their point of view and their answers give great insight into what kids like.'

Design Heroes: Tammis Keefe, Marimekko (see pages 204–7), Pucci

Favourite Children's Illustrators: Charley Harper, William Joyce

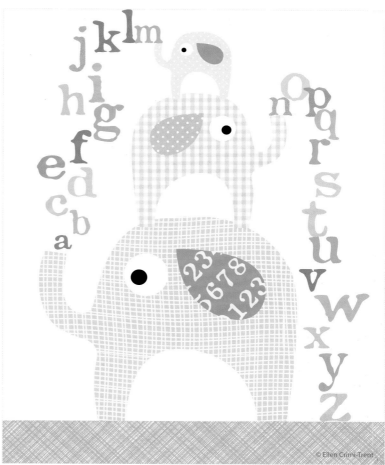

© Ellen Crimi-Trent

Left / Spring Lane
Colourful houses occupy
a lane filled with flowers,
trees, and butterflies in this
idealized town. The fine,
ornate fences add a touch
of retro appeal. Created with
nursery bedding in mind.

Above / Le Petit Eléphant
A stack is a classic device
for illustrating lots of animals
in a fun way. Here Ellen has
filled each elephant with a
different pattern. Created
as part of a co-ordinating
collection for potential
licensing clients.

Esther Hall

www.owlandcatdesigns.co.uk
esther@owlandcatdesigns.co.uk

33 // ˙ Esther Hall is based in Lancashire, UK. She originally studied Textile Design at Nottingham University. Then, after owning her own shop selling children's furniture and accessories, and having children, she went back to study an MA in Children's Book Illustration at The University of Central Lancashire. Esther had her first book published by Pan Macmillan in 2011 and has also illustrated books for a Korean publisher. Her work is influenced by her textile design background, in particular 1950s textile design. She also loves the colours and graphic style of 1950s Czech film posters. Esther's website and online shop Owl and Cat Designs came as an offshoot to her textile design work. She began selling prints of her illustrations before going on to design her first range of products. Esther says her ambition now is to just keep expanding her business, concentrating on designing products for children, and widening her audience by selling wholesale to independent retailers.

Design Heroes: Lucienne Day, Orla Kiely (see pages 232–3), Ella Doran

Favourite Children's Illustrators: Bruno Munari, Adrian Johnson, Marc Boutavant (see pages 196–9)

Top left / Owl and Cat Went to Sea
Esther's owl and pussycat characters have been placed in their classic 'pea green boat' for this lino-print design created for a children's print.

Top right / Lil and Flip
The two characters Lil and Flip were an idea for a children's picture book initially, but Esther thought they would make a lovely print. The original design was created using lino-printing.

Bottom / Colin Crocodile
One of a set of animal designs for Esther's first range of children's cards. The coloured triangles on the crocodile's back offer a chance to add colour.

ferm LIVING

www.ferm-living.com
info@ferm-living.com

34 //   ferm LIVING is a Danish company that originally began as a graphic design agency but later moved into designing and manufacturing interior products with a graphic touch. The inspiration to launch ferm LIVING came in 2005 when the company's founder, Trine Andersen, could not find affordable graphic wallpaper to decorate her house. She decided to create her own designs and the first collection was launched in 2006. Since then the ferm LIVING product range has expanded into wall stickers, textiles, kitchen items, and of course a large 'KIDS collection'. When selling to young children designers need to capture the attention of style-conscious parents first, which is something ferm LIVING have easily achieved. The company's philosophy is to create a children's room that is a sanctuary in which they can enjoy countless hours of happy and imaginative play.

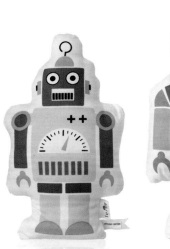

Top / The Village Cushion
An organic-cotton shaped cushion featuring a house motif from The Village wallpaper. This design is one of four different designs allowing children to create their own street.

Bottom / Mr Small and Mr Large
Friendly robots are printed onto organic cotton for these boys' shaped cushions. The flat-coloured, bold graphics make them great bedtime companions, or according to ferm, fun for pillow fights!

Opposite / Tiny Train
A fabulous retro-style wallpaper that is both fun for little ones and aesthetically pleasing to adults. For this design, featuring a train of elephants, ferm LIVING have used a vintage texture effect to give the motifs a subtle distressed look.

Opposite / The Village
This architectural wallpaper depicting a charming village has the wonderful Scandinavian appeal of clean lines and simple graphics. Shown here in coral, blue, grey, and pink.

Above / Kids' Textiles
A selection of stylish children's textiles from ferm LIVING look fabulous when piled up together en masse. Creating a range of designs that can happily mix and match ensures customers can keep adding to their collection.

Filipa Cipriano

fciprianodesign.blogspot.com
fcbcipriano@gmail.com
rep: www.mysugarcube.com

35 // Filipa Cipriano is originally from Portugal but is currently based in London. Filipa studied Fashion/Textiles Design and Business Studies at Brighton University, UK. During this time she had the opportunity to do a year internship in Milan, New York, and India. For the last six years Filipa has worked for the My Sugar Cube design studio where she has really been able to develop her passion for childrenswear design and pattern, as well as the sales side of the business. Clients have included Babies R Us, Macy's, Accessorize, Sainsbury's, Pumpkin Patch and Debenhams. Filipa's main design passion comes from colour and textiles, especially from India, Africa, and South American cultures. She also loves the vintage and modern illustrations in children's books and packaging. Filipa would love to do a commission for anyone who likes her work, but says one day she would like to have her own line of print designs for women's and children's fashion and home interiors.

Design Heroes: Frida Kahlo, Celia Birtwell, Jean-Michel Basquiat

Favourite Children's Illustrators: Miroslav Sasek, Catimini

Opposite top / Happy Woodland
This magical forest design brimming with colour and movement was created in Adobe Illustrator, for the Turner Bianca design studio, for children's bedding.

Opposite bottom / Little Captain
A fabulously textured graphic placement print with adventurous typography which was used on boys' clothing. Created in Adobe Illustrator using a crayon effect. Created for My Sugar Cube design studio.

Above / Trees
Graphic lollipop trees interlock for maximum coverage in this girls' print design, which was created in Adobe Illustrator for My Sugar Cube design studio. Some of the imagery was hand-drawn and then taken into Adobe Illustrator for finishing.

Flora Waycott

www.florawaycottdesign.com

36 // Flora Waycott is originally from England, with an English father and a Japanese mother. She spent her childhood growing up in Japan, which is where a lot of her design influences have come from. Flora studied Textile Design at Winchester School of Art in the UK, but during her degree lived in Kyoto for four months whilst learning the art of Japanese crafts. Currently based in Wellington, New Zealand, Flora freelances for a textile design studio in London, creating prints and embroideries for childrenswear. She also works as a university tutor. Her inspiration comes from a love of the simplicity and cleanliness of Scandinavian design, Japanese prints and patterns, stationery, children's books, spots and stripes, old kokeshi dolls, vintage fabrics with bold, colourful designs, vintage tea towels, and colours in different countries (colours on the side of buildings, food, fruit, markets, etc). Flora has had greetings cards published by The Art Group, and would one day love to have her own product range with her designs on anything from stationery to mugs and cups to clothing.

Design Heroes: Marimekko (see pages 204–7), Shinzi Katoh, Celia Birtwell

Favourite Children's Illustrators: Retta Worcester, Eric Carle, Dick Bruna

Opposite top / Friendly Flowers
These flowers instantly become friendly when faces are added and give a cute, fun, and happy look to this design for girls. All individually hand-drawn, scanned, and digitally coloured.

Opposite bottom / Ribbons in Bows
A fabulous fashion print for girls of all ages. Flora loves ribbons, especially how the cute shape of a bow looks as a detail. She cleverly uses a mix of outlined bows and solid colours for this sweet repeat. Hand-drawn, scanned, and digitally coloured.

Above / My Home
Inspired by the interesting and unique houses on the hillsides of Wellington, New Zealand. Flora has also included other aspects of her home such as her cat Shima and her little garden. Hand-drawn, scanned, and digitally coloured.

Gail Veillette

www.gailveillette.com
www.gailveillette.blogspot.com
gailveillette@gmail.com

37 // Gail Veillette is originally from Connecticut, in the US, but is now based in Florida. She studied Illustration at Ringling College of Art and Design. Gail has always been inspired by animation and children's books and lately has also been looking at interior design, fashion, and sculpture for inspiration. Gail began her career working for a baby clothing company before deciding to pursue a freelance career working in the childrenswear and stationery fields. In the future, Gail would love to illustrate children's books and design a line of toys.

Design Heroes: Alexander Girard, Ronald Searle, Maira Kalman

Favourite Children's Illustrators: Alice and Martin Provensen, Mary Blair, Marc Boutavant (see pages 196–9)

Left / Sketchbook Pattern
This bold animal pattern would be great for babies and toddlers. It was created using a variety of sketchbook drawings. For the final pattern, Gail focused on shape and colour and tried to simplify the sketches as much as possible.

Top / Cat Garden
A wonderful, whimsical pattern that is saturated with happy colour and cute-eyed cats inspired by Gail's cat, Harrison. All works were done digitally, although a lot of Gail's designs will start with a sketch on a scrap of paper.

Bottom / Hello
A placement print designed as a companion graphic for the Cat Garden repeat pattern. Created originally with note cards in mind as a self-initiated project to build her portfolio.

Haciendo el Indio

www.haciendoelindio.com
www.haciendoelindio.bigcartel.com
info@haciendoelindio.com

38 // Haciendo el Indio is a Spanish company that creates beautiful and enduring products for children. Its founder, creator, and designer Cristina Serrano is originally from Madrid, but currently the business is based in Valencia. Cristina studied at Ecole Parsons in Paris and Central Saint Martins in London. Haciendo el Indio's range includes wall prints, textiles, and dolls, and they will also happily take on design, decoration, and illustration commissions from other companies and clients. Cristina's illustrations are inspired by nature, art, music, travelling, and childhood. Cristina found having her son and daughter made her travel back to her own childhood and rediscover the magic of nature, animals, playing, and 'childish' things in general. In the future Cristina would love to design wall art murals and her dream would be to decorate an art museum for children.

Design Heroes: Eva Zeisel, Charles and Ray Eames, Enzo Mari

Favourite Children's Illustrator: Sara Fanelli

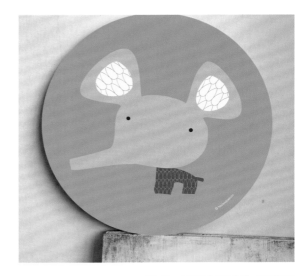

Opposite top, middle & bottom /
Round Wall Art
A selection of circular vector illustrations printed and mounted on a wood fibre panel for easy hanging. Featuring an elephant, a lion, and a sweet rabbit resplendent in bold, flared trousers, looks out from this round wood-mounted print.

Top / Circus
A stylish circus print featuring a sophisticated muted grey background and a highly ornate typeface. Sold as prints or wall hangings at Haciendo el Indio.

Bottom / Squirrel and House
Cristina's aim is to create designs to fill any room with happiness and imagination, just like this illustration of a squirrel carrying his acorn, and a little house with a tree.

Helen Dardik

www.orangeyoulucky.blogspot.com
www.lillarogers.com/artists/helen-dardik
info@lillarogers.com

39 // Helen Dardik is originally from Odessa in the Ukraine but is now based in Ottawa, Canada. She studied at the ORT School of Art & Design in Israel, and later studied Graphic Design in Canada. Her inspiration comes from illustrated children's books that Helen read over and over again as a child. These Norwegian fairytales and Russian folk stories inspire her still. Anything that exudes colourful, playful innocence inspires Helen and she loves random colours that go together. Clients have included Target, Blue Q, Chronicle Books, Gallison/Mudpuppy, Madison Park, Hallmark, Mara-Mi and many more. Helen's dream commission would be to design some large-scale fabric and illustrate ceramic tiles and dishes. Her ambitions for the future include opening her own stationery shop, and writing-illustrating some children's books, either traditionally printed or as digital downloads. Helen currently concentrates on illustration and surface design and is represented by top US design agency Lilla Rogers.

Design Heroes: Alexander Girard, Saul Steinberg, Stig Lindberg

Favourite Children's Illustrators: Abner Graboff, Taro Gomi, Mary Blair

Top left / Hello Summer
A fun and colourful illustration where Helen uses her own exuberant style. Her whimsical rendering of people is almost cartoon-like, with thin bendy arms and tiny feet. Created in 2012 for personal work.

Top right / Hooray for Birthdays: Tiger
The way Helen illustrates her characters is with more of a fantastical approach rather than a realistic one. This adorable tiger has a smiling, friendly face which is sure to appeal to children and fire their imagination.

Bottom left / Bestest Friends
Helen illustrated this delightful duo as a limited edition giclée print to sell in her Etsy Shop. Her illustration style is contemporary in feeling but with a whimsical fairytale quality. Created in 2012 for personal work.

Bottom right /
Hooray for Birthdays: Dog
A sense of fun prevails throughout the whole Hooray for Birthdays collection. This jaunty dog character sports his smartest clothes and is showered in a confetti of colourful dots creating a playful, happy feel.

the BESTEST FRIENDS

Hikje

www.hikje.com
www.plaksels.nl
janneke@hikje.com

40 // 'Hikje' means 'little hiccup' in Dutch. It is the studio label for designer Janneke Zantinge who is based in Groningen, The Netherlands. Janneke studied Product Design at Utrecht School of the Arts. After Janneke's son was born in 2010 she realized that her ambition had shifted from being a product designer to being an illustrator. She turned in her workshop and bought an iMac. Janneke designed her son's birth announcement and was soon asked to design some more for a birth announcement company. This was the start of her career as an illustrator. As she had studied product design, Janneke's work is strongly influenced by this genre, but also by architecture and comic books. Her ideal commission would be to make a series of stop-motion films for a program like Sesame Street.

Design Heroes: Studio Job, Hundertwasser, Tim Burton

Favourite Children's Illustrators: Dick Bruna, Eric Carle

Opposite top / Vinyl Wall Decal: Cars
Janneke also has her own label
called Plaksels which produces
vinyl wall decorations. These graphic
transport motifs are classic subject
matter for boys.

Opposite middle /
Birth Announcement: Flower
A scan of gingham fabric makes a great
contrast with the flat graphic flowers.
A semi-opaque white heart ensures the
child's name will stand out. Designed
for birth announcement company Lief
Leuk & Eigen. www.liefleukeneigen.nl

Opposite bottom /
Birth Announcement: Blocks
Traditional building blocks are
an iconic image of childhood and
look great set against blue gingham
in this design created for birth
announcement company Lief Leuk
& Eigen. www.liefleukeneigen.nl

Top left / Hedgehog Postcard
From the Hikje ABC Series. Janneke's
postcards have a fabulous background
of multicoloured dots. The dots are
cleverly kept to white only behind
the animal motifs to ensure they are
framed by, rather than lost in, the
lively pattern.

Top right / Crocodile Postcard
From the Hikje ABC Series. Janneke
is very adept at making her animal
characters look friendly – even
this crocodile would make a cute
companion. Offset-printed on heavy
card stock.

Left / ABC Poster
From the Hikje ABC Series. This
A2-sized poster is both educational
and decorative as each animal is
accompanied by a little letter.

I'd like to be...

www.idliketobe.com
jamienashillustration.blogspot.co.uk
hello@idliketobe.com

41 // Jamie Nash is the designer and illustrator behind 'I'd like to be...'. Originally from Yorkshire, Jamie studied a degree in Graphic Design at Northumbria University and now bases himself in London. Before setting up 'I'd like to be...', Jamie created designs for Cadbury Buttons, Green & Black's Explorers, Jamie Oliver, and The Natural Confectionery Co. Jamie often finds inspiration from vintage children's storybooks and toys. He then interprets these influences to give them a modern edge. Going forward he would love to develop the 'I'd like to be...' range and expand into home and fashion accessories.

Design Heroes: Alexander Girard, Charley Harper, Paul Rand

Favourite Children's Illustrator: Raymond Briggs

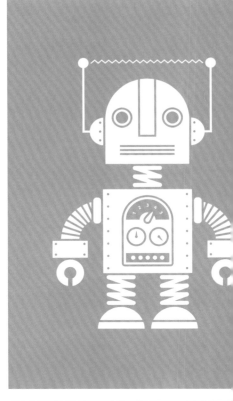

All & overleaf / A Space Robot, A Racing Car Driver, A Prima Ballerina, A Creative Cook, A Shootin' Sheriff, A Policeman, A Red Bus Driver, A Noble Knight
Each design in the 'I'd like to be...' series is silkscreen-printed onto 240gsm Sirio paper. The series concept evokes a simpler time when we wished we could be a brave knight or a shiny space robot from outer space. The designs have a bold and distinctive style and feature one-colour backgrounds with white characters.

A series of illustrated characters that answer the age-old question, 'What would you like to be?' Jamie says he believes in making beautifully simple and crafted designs that would be striking in any home. At 'I'd like to be...' they produce the illustrations as hand-pulled screen-prints that will appeal to design-conscious parents.

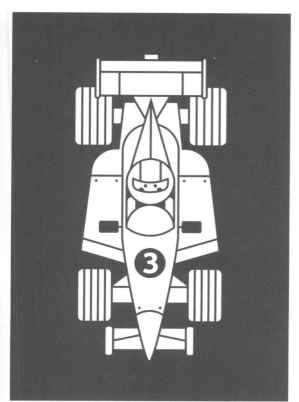

Ian Dutton

www.ianduttondesigns.com
ian@ianduttondesigns.com

42 // Ian Dutton is based in Stockton-on-Tees in the UK. He studied a BA(Hons) in Graphic Arts and Design at Leeds Metropolitan University. Ian specializes in character design and development, together with illustration and surface design. Clients have included Marks & Spencer, Next, Mamas & Papas, Boots, WHSmith, The Early Learning Centre, Hallmark, and Mothercare. Ian has also won a prestigious Henries award for a Christmas card design and a Mother and Baby silver award for best children's toy. He finds his biggest inspiration comes from seeing other people happy and inspired by his illustrations, especially children, who have the most amazing imaginations and provide Ian with a great source of amusement, which he hopes shows through in his drawings. In 2011 Ian was invited to Calgary, Canada, to work as an artist-in-residence at Millarville Community School. One day Ian would really like to make his characters move and would love to make a short animation. His dream would be to get a chance to work with his design superhero, Adrian Johnson.

Design Heroes: Adrian Johnson, Delphine Durand, David Sheldon

Favourite Children's Illustrators: Otto Seibold, Oliver Jeffers

Top / Elephant Parade
A fun-packed illustration that demonstrates Ian's skill at creating characters for young children. Buttons for wheels and comical hats are just some of the appealing features included, and the typography and harlequin patterns show he keeps up with trends. Client: Mamas & Papas.

Bottom / Whoosh Jumbo
Ian is very confident at mixing typography with his illustration work. Here the lettering is formed from clouds around a stylized jumbo jet. Client: UK Greetings for Asda.

Left /
'I like rain,' said Mr Elephant
Although this is a digital design, Ian has still managed to get lots of texture into the image and play with the opacities. There is also a good balance between delicate lines and scribbles and chunkier, bolder strokes. Client: UK Greetings for Tesco.

Below /
'I'm happy,' said Mr Lion
This colourful lion has a hand-printed look thanks to clever use of digital illustration. The striking geometric mane and friendly face form the centrepiece for this design that turns a wild animal into a child's cutest companion. Client: UK Greetings For Tesco.

IKEA

www.ikea.com

43 // IKEA was founded in Sweden in 1943 by 17-year-old Ingvar Kamprad, and opened its first store in 1953. Since then it has grown to become a global brand with close to 340 stores worldwide. IKEA's children's designs are bright, durable, and functional and created to stimulate young minds and bring extra colour and fun to their lives. Their distinctive Scandinavian style can be found on children's furniture, bedding, tableware, lighting, and toys. IKEA's stores are also designed with children in mind and most stores have a special play area, named 'Småland' (Swedish for 'small land') where children can be dropped off to have fun while parents do their shopping. For well-designed products at great prices you can always rely on IKEA as the designs included here show.

Top /
Vitaminer Vimpel (Bunting)
© Inter IKEA Systems B.V
This IKEA design by Sirpa Cowell is perfect for both boys or girls thanks to its rainbow palette and graphic simplicity. Shown here on bedlinen that will engage any child at bedtime.

Bottom /
Vitaminer Trumma (Drums)
© Inter IKEA Systems B.V
Another playful print designed by Sirpa Cowell is featured here on bedlinen and is full of joy and movement. The drumsticks arranged in different positions make it almost seem animated.

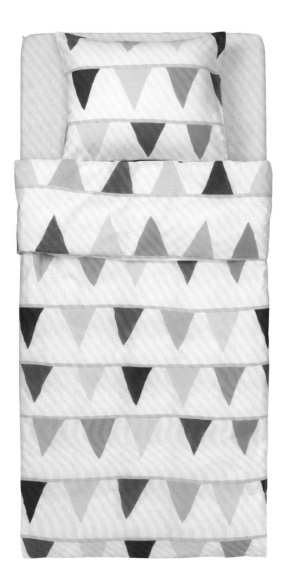

Right / Barnslig Dans
© Inter IKEA Systems B.V
Bedlinen by Eva Lundgreen.
For this design Eva says
she wasn't interested in
capturing reality as it is,
but as it might look in a
child's imagination. 'Barnslig'
means 'childish' in Swedish.

Below / Barnslig
© Inter IKEA Systems B.V
For this range of fabrics
Barnslig's designer
Eva Lundgreen wanted
to make children happy,
as well as stimulate their
imagination and creativity
with stylized shapes and
contrasting colours.

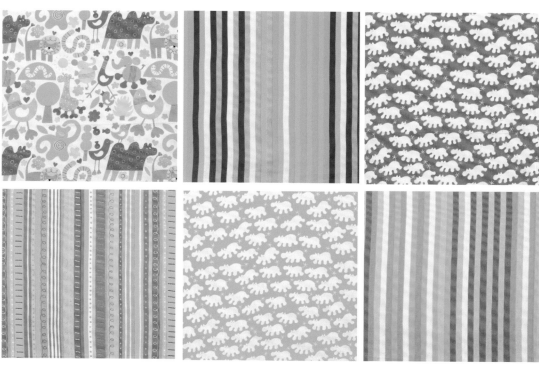

Opposite / Vitaminer Bil (Cars)
This transport print designed by Sirpa Cowell is bright and colourful but manages to keep a light and airy feel by using outline for all the vehicles and only using solid colour for the tyres.

Top / Vitaminer Hjarta (Hearts)
A pattern perfect for girls of all ages that maintains the bold graphic IKEA aesthetic whilst still looking pretty and feminine at the same time. Designed by Sirpa Cowell.

Bottom / Vitaminer Leksak (Mixed)
A non-directional print packed with little motifs to capture the imagination. The motifs are outlined in contrasting colours and are suitable for both genders. Designed by Sirpa Cowell.

Ingela P. Arrhenius

www.ingelaparrhenius.com
hello@ingelaparrhenius.com

₄₄ // Ingela P. Arrhenius is a well-known and popular illustrator who was born in the Netherlands but moved to Sweden when she was just two years old. Ingela studied Graphic Design at the Berghs School of Communication in Stockholm, and now lives just outside the city in a suburb called Enskede where she works as a freelance illustrator. Her work includes advertising, packaging, greetings cards, book illustrations, toys, and much more. Recently Ingela has created designs for a range of toiletries for Biotherm. Clients have included Paperchase, The Swedish Post Office, Bookbinders, London 2012, and Lagom. Ingela finds her inspiration in scouring flea markets and collecting vintage children's books. For the future she would like to design porcelain figurines as she really enjoys working in 3D, and would also like to create designs for wallpaper. Ingela has agents in Sweden (Soderberg Agentur), Germany (kombinatrotweiss), the US (Snyder) and the UK (Pepper Cookies).

Design Heroes: Lisa Larsson, Olle Eksell, Stig Lindberg

Favourite Children's Illustrators: Åke Lewerth, Lili Scratchy

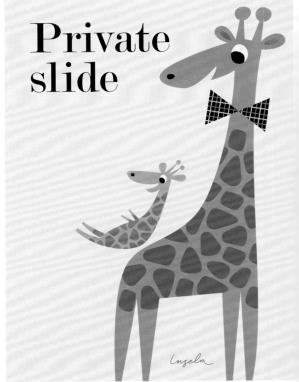

Ingela P Arrhenius

Jag vet!

VI KLÄR PÅ OSS

Ingela P Arrhenius VI KLÄR PÅ OSS

Ingela P Arrhenius

Jag vet!

VI ÄTER MAT

Ingela P Arrhenius VI ÄTER MAT

Opposite top / Lion
Ingela's lion poster for OMM Design has a retro appeal reflecting her love of '50s and '60s design. This beautiful design is sophisticated enough to appeal to adults and children alike.

Opposite bottom / Giraffe
Artwork created for Fab.com. This poster design, with a baby giraffe sliding down its parent's back, exudes fun and movement. The design has a mid-century modern flavour but with a contemporary twist.

Top left / I Know! We Get Dressed
Board book published by Rabén & Sjögren. Ingela's irresistible animals, like this fox putting on his mittens, make the subject of getting dressed appealing to babies.

Top right / I Know! We Eat
Board book published by Rabén & Sjögren especially for babies. Featuring Ingela's clear and colourful designs to explain the subject of eating. Sweet designs like this tiger getting to grips with spaghetti absolutely sparkle with charm.

Bottom left / Duka Kids
Ingela created this 'Kids' Collection' of melamine products for Polish company Duka. Perfect for brightening up children's mealtimes as Ingela's characters prepare your toddler's favourite dish.

Bottom right / Nesting Dolls
Products for OMM Design.
A set of six animal dolls who fit snugly inside each other.

Isa Form

www.isa.nu
info@isa.nu

45 // Isabelle Norman Sällström is a freelance graphic designer and illustrator who runs the Isa Form printshop based in Piteå, Sweden. Isabelle studied Design and Illustration at Berghs School of Communication in Stockholm, and she once represented Sweden in a graphic design competition. This took her to Seoul in Korea and gave her a terrific confidence boost. Isabelle's clients have included Skip Hop, Voksi, Unicef, TePe, Spira Inredning, and FinnUpp. She loves 1950s-style design and finds inspiration in children and their drawings and expressions. She is the mother of two boys and says her eldest son draws a lot and has probably inherited her creative side. She gets very inspired by him and his various phases: 'When he was in his superhero phase of course I made a superhero print!' Isabelle has always dreamed about making children's books. 'I have so many ideas,' she says. 'But not the knowledge and connections to make them real.'

Design Heroes: Stig Lindberg, Charles and Ray Eames, Arne Jacobsen

Favourite Children's Illustrators: Poul Ströyer, Lasse Sandberg, Stina Wirsén

Top / Castle
'I fancy things with a '50s vibe, and I think it shows in my drawings!' says Isabelle, and it is certainly true of this modernistic castle illustration. Sold as a personalized print, the child's name (or anything else) can be written in the castle's flag.

Bottom / Cute Crocodile
A unifying element in Isabelle's square animals prints is the multicoloured triangle forms, which are cleverly used here on the crocodile's teeth and spine.

HERE LIVE A FELLOW NAMED ADAM

Zoey

Milton

Alice

Top left / Apple of My Eye
Red contrasts beautifully
with pink on this apple art
print. The skeletal black
linework of the leaves and
the scripted text make a
great balance with the solid
colour of the apple.

Top right / City Street
This colourful city is a great
way to bring mid-century
modern style graphics
to a child's nursery. The
buildings, water, and sun
have a geometric structure
and the cars add a more
whimsical touch.

Middle left / Clumsy Owl
Here Isabelle has pared
down the characteristics
of an owl with clarity and
simplicity. The feathers
are represented by simple
triangles.

Middle right / Clever Dach
A bouncing sausage dog
in a colourful sweater
makes this a very lively
and dynamic name print.

Bottom / Calm Cat
This cat is very content with
its rainbow coat of triangles
and stripes.

Isak

www.isak.co.uk
www.sandraisaksson.com
sandra@sandraisaksson.com

46 // Sandra Isaksson is the designer and owner of Isak. Sandra is originally from Sweden but now lives in West Sussex, in the UK. She studied a Masters degree in Graphic Design and Illustration in Denmark, and as well as running the business and designing for Isak, Sandra also takes on freelance work and commissions. Her clients have included Marks & Spencer, Skip Hop, teNeues and Case Scenario. Sandra's work is influenced by her Scandinavian heritage, and she is inspired by design from 1950 to 1970, as well as people, travelling, and her children. 'The kids' products I design, I design for them,' she says. Sandra's ambition would be to create children's books, and to work more with product design and clothing.

Design Heroes: Olle Eksell, Charley Harper, Stig Lindberg

Favourite Children's Illustrators: Alain Grée (see pages 10–15), Sven Nordqvist

Top / 123 Workboard
Opposite / ABC Workboard
Printed onto Scandinavian hardboard, these alphabet and number prints are designed to be both educational and decorative. The wall decorations are made in Sweden using wood from sustainable sources and because of their protective coating are truly interactive and fun. Children can learn from them, eat on them, draw on them – and then just wipe them clean and put them back on the wall.

Bottom / Workboards Photo
These sturdy boards can stand up on their own, meaning they can be easily moved around the nursery without the need for wall fixing.

0 1 2 3 4 5 6 7 8 9 10 11 12 13 14 15 16 17 18 19 20

Top / Penguin Wallpapers
Rolls of Penguin wallpaper available in a fabulous selection of cool Scandinavian colours: wasabi green, plum pink, silver, and turquoise.

Bottom / ABC and 123 Prints
Beautiful interactive posters to make counting and learning the alphabet fun. There are lots of animals, birds, trees, and pattern fills to create interest. Sandra creates most of her designs in Adobe Illustrator. The posters are then litho-printed in England with vegetable inks.

Opposite / Penguin
For this penguin motif only the details actually necessary to indicate that it is a bird have been included, creating a beautifully fresh and simple pattern. Shown here in wasabi green, this design features on wallpaper, bedlinen and blankets.

Jay-Cyn Designs

www.birchfabrics.com
www.fabricworm.com
cynthia@birchfabrics.com

47 // Jay-Cyn Designs are a husband-and-wife team comprised of Jason Rector and Cynthia Mann. The Californian couple met and married in San Francisco but now live in Paso Robles. Cynthia studied Fashion and Textiles at San Francisco State University, and Jason studied Multimedia Design and CEA & ICDA in San Francisco. Cynthia opened Fabricworm.com, an online shop for modern print fabrics, in 2008 and, not long after, she started Birch Fabrics when she noticed that the modern fabric community was lacking in organic options. Together with Jason they became Jay-Cyn Designs and began designing their own fabrics with modern children's illustrations and graphics. Their influences come from a love of mid-century and Japanese design. Their first collection, Avalon, was released in June 2010 and they have since designed many more collections for Birch Fabrics with great success. Jay-Cyn Designs is open to design commissions from other companies. Their dream job would be to design patterns for a line of children's bedding.

Design Heroes: Alexander Girard, Lotta Jansdotter, Etsuko Furuya

Favourite Children's Illustrators: Dan Stiles (see page 84-7), Charley Harper, Monaluna

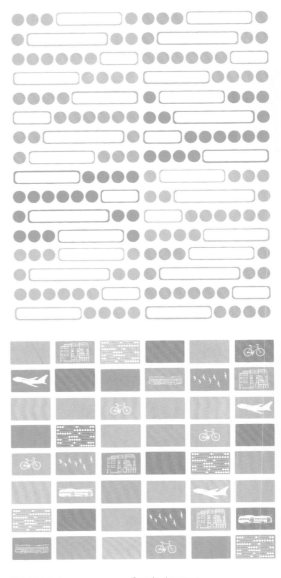

Top / Gridlock
A fun, abstracted, geometric design that is great for mixing and blending with the more pictorial fabrics in the Commute collection. The playful look of the dots and squares makes it ideal for a nursery or playroom.

Bottom / City Block
Transport is always a popular theme for boys and this design uses masculine colours and a geometric structure. It was created using a mixture of hand-drawn and computer-illustrated design for the Birch Fabrics Commute collection.

Opposite / To Work
A hand-drawn and computer-illustrated design featuring a bustling city of planes and bicycles. Part of the Birch Fabrics Commute collection, all of which are printed on 100 per cent premium certified organic cotton.

Jayne Schofield

www.jayneschofield.blogspot.com
www.thatsmyfolio.com/folio/Jayne-Schofield
jaydoug@scho4.wanadoo.co.uk

48 // Jayne Schofield is originally from Lancashire but lived and worked all around the world before eventually settling back in the north west of England. Jayne began by studying Graphic Design at Staffordshire University but moved onto the Illustration degree course half way through. This gave her a love of mixing illustration and text together in her designs. Her design inspiration and influences come from her little boy Ben, artists Matisse and David Hockney, text and words, nature and animals, and travel. Clients have included WHSmith, Just Kids Ltd, Paper Magic and Design Design. As well as design, Jayne would love to work in the field of children's picture book illustration.

Design Heroes: Jill McDonald, Carolyn Gavin (see pages 100–3), Sara Fanelli

Favourite Children's Illustrators: Lauren Child, Clare Fennell, Mary Mcquillan

Top / Life's a Hoot
This wide-eyed owl was hand-drawn and scanned in; Jayne then built up the image using transparent layers, starting with the grid background. Stitching was added to give texture while the jaunty, angular typography adds rhythm and interest.

Bottom / Time for Bed
A quick piece of illustration produced for Jayne's blog to illustrate how poorly she felt when she had the flu. It is made up of a digital collage using scanned fabric, cut out lettering and freehand drawing using a tablet.

Left / Lion
This image was produced as part of a collection of ideas for Jayne's appliqué zoo animals series. Created using tablet freehand drawing and digital collage. The body has the look of being cut from coloured paper whilst the mane, in contrast, has a loose doodle feel.

Below / On the Move
Digital design. Each individual element was hand-drawn and scanned in. Jayne then arranged them in a composition using digital collage techniques. She chose a soft palette to suit the nursery and added stitching, buttons, and fabric to create a textile feel. 'I like to play with text and words in my work to add another dimension and to give it a playful feel,' she says.

Jillian Phillips

jillyp.co.uk
jillypgraphics.blogspot.co.uk
jillygraphics@yahoo.co.uk
Rep: www.lillarogers.com

49 // Jillian Phillips from Wimborne in Dorset studied Fashion Design for four years, but found out pretty quickly that she preferred designing the fabric to the garment. Jillian works as a freelance designer and is one of the artists represented by the renowned Lilla Rogers Studio (www.lillarogers.com). Clients have included Paperchase, Galison, Fisher Price, Mothercare, The Land of Nod, Gap, Target, and Madison Park Greetings, for whom Jillian won a prestigious Louis Award in 2012. Jillian is inspired by shopping trips to Tokyo, and vintage kids books, flea market finds, New York, and the other Lilla Rogers artists. All the artworks here were pieces created for Jillian's Lilla Rogers Studio collection with a view to being sold at print shows such as Surtex and Printsource. Jillian's dream would be to have her own brand of stationery, greetings cards, fabrics and more! 'It's what keeps me working hard,' she says.

Design Heroes: Charley Harper, Shinzi Katoh

Favourite Children's Illustrator: Richard Scarry

Top / Dog Loves Flower
An assortment of fuzzy dogs wearing clothes is typical of Jillian's quirky and whimsical style. Each adorable dog is peppered with colourful flowers and the whole design is held together on a gridded background. Created in Adobe Illustrator and licensed to Madison Park Greetings.

Bottom / Animal Mix Zoo
Animals and zoos provide an endless source of inspiration for children's designers and are useful as they can appeal to both boys and girls. This design, however, is sweetly feminine and delicate. Created for use on baby wrapping paper and greetings cards.

Above / Cut and Sew Pets
These adorable characters exemplify Jillian's wonderful
ability to create cute heart-warming design. Clever use
of pattern and a sophisticated colour scheme also give it
adult appeal. Created for use on stationery at Paperchase.
Design copyright of Paperchase.

Opposite / Mouse Village
Jillian's ability to depict her animals and characters with such soft, charming faces makes them perfect for very young children or babies. This jolly village design was hand-drawn, and then scanned in. Jillian imagined these characters possibly being used in a book.

Above / May Bunny
This design, which was created for fabric and stationery, was developed from a gouache painting experiment. Blocks of colour are used for the motifs and black linework fills in the details.

June Craft

www.junecraft.com
junecraft@gmail.com

50 // June Craft is the design label of Kayanna Nelson from Cedar Rapids, Iowa. Kayanna is mostly self-taught and finds she is constantly learning from her peers as well, which she says is 'the best kind of education!' Kayanna currently works as a full-time art director for a Chicago-based advertising agency. She creates packaging and advertising for large retail businesses. She has been designing her own prints and patterns for sale on Etsy and Spoonflower but the 'Hey! That's Swell' collection for Cloud 9 is her first foray into licensing designs for a fabric company and she has loved every minute of it. Moving forward, Kayanna really wants to continue to create designs for licensing on fabric. 'That's my dream job,' she says, 'and I hope one day to be able to be completely self-employed.'

Design Heroes: Heather Ross, Skinny LaMinx (Heather Moore), Lotta Jansdotter

Favourite Children's Illustrators: Mary Blair, Jim Flora

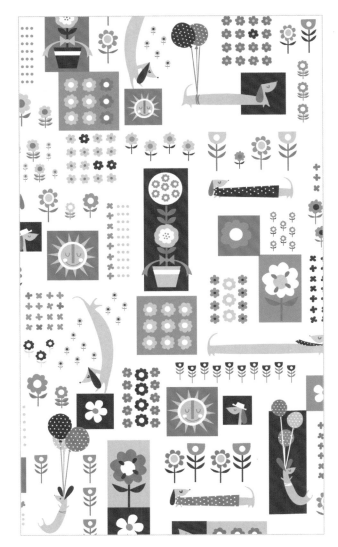

Above / Long Dogs
Here the dogs and flowers are arranged on a geometric structure, meaning all their fabric designs can sit next to each other without clashing.

Opposite top / Right On Angles
This design is very modernistic and bold, but the overall colour coverage means it will look great alongside lighter prints in the collection.

Opposite bottom /
Sweet and Swell Floral
Through Kayanna's use of layering this retro floral design appears to have lots of depth.

Overleaf /
Super Swell Patchwork
This is the one fabric in the collection that brings all the motifs together in one pattern.

Kara White

www.krop.com/karawhite
www.karawhitedesign.blogspot.com
kara@karawhitedesign.co.uk

51 // Kara White is originally from Oxfordshire, UK, and was inspired by her art teacher Mr. Childs to pursue design as a career. Kara studied a BSc in Textile Design at the University of Huddersfield and has designed for many UK high street shops as well as retailers in the US, Australia, and Japan. She works with two studios, Paper & Cloth and Elizabeth Stirling Designs. Kara adores using colour and creating patterns and cute characters. Her inspiration comes from many different, amazing people and things – from looking at blogs, trends and books, seeing something in the garden or on a walk, or from a special find in a junk shop. Kara's ambition is to one day illustrate a children's book.

Design Heroes: Henri Matisse, Helen Dardik (see pages 128–31), Orla Kiely (see pages 232–3)

Favourite Children's Illustrators: Yara Kono, Nicola Killen, Mary Blair

Top / It's Raining Cats and Dogs
Here Kara has taken a quirky British saying and turned it into a fun print. The scattered design is full of textures, effects, and squiggles. The stylized rain is made from various confetti-like geometrics.

Bottom / Animal Magic
A very lively print featuring animals, flowers, numbers, and textures is toned down for babies by using a calming grey and green palette. Kara's original hand-drawn sketches were scanned in and then traced over in Adobe Illustrator, with colour, texture, and pattern added. The design features as both a repeating pattern and a placement print.

Opposite / Retro Jungle
This fabulous two-colour print features wonderfully cute animals whose details and features have been added by lots and lots of little dots. Created from hand-drawn sketches scanned in and then drawn over digitally.

Kate Legge

www.katelegge.com
www.maplejack.etsy.com
katelegge@live.com

52 // Kate Legge was born in Bristol, England, and raised in Vancouver, British Columbia, Canada. She studied Graphic Design at Kwantlen Polytechnic University before working as a graphic/textile designer for a national Canadian children's clothing company for six years. This is where Kate developed a love of print design and honed her illustration skills for the children's market. She currently works as a freelance graphic and textile designer and loves to search for inspiration in bookshops and libraries. Kate likes anything that feels modern and fresh but with a retro touch and is especially influenced by mid-century design and Scandinavian textiles. Her son has been a big influence on her recent design work. Kate discovered Spoonflower when looking for ways to print custom bedding for his crib. This lead to her opening an Etsy store (called Maple Jack) that provides modern but playful textiles and graphic art prints for nurseries. Kate's dream commission would be to design babies' bedding for Dwell Studio.

Design Heroes: Dwell Studio, Orla Kiely (see pages 232–3), Alexander Girard

Favourite Children's Illustrators: Oliver Jeffers, Alison Oliver, Mary Blair

Opposite top / Scoops
This print is inspired by
the delicious colours of
Italian ice cream, gelato.
Kate wanted to create a
playful alternative to the
classic polka dot print.
All of the designs are based
on pencil sketches that are
re-drawn, coloured and
formatted in Illustrator.

Opposite bottom /
Pizza Wedges
A geometric take on the
pizza. Colour blocking
the wedges gives the print
almost an optical feel of
depth and texture. The
delicious pastel palette
makes it perfect for use
in nursery decor. Originally
designed for Kate's Etsy
store and for purchase
on Spoonflower.

Top / Roma
This is Kate's primary print
in a textile collection called
Roman Holiday, which was
inspired by vintage Italian
graphic design, the city
of Rome and the colours
of gelato. With its sunny
Mediterranean feel, it was
designed primarily for baby
girl blankets.

Bottom / Roman Stripe
Ice cream colours make
up this pretty but simple
co-ordinate fabric which
is ideal for blending with
other designs in the
Roman Holiday collection.
The collection was designed
with baby girls in mind
and a boys' collection
with a London theme
is also available.

Ketchup on
Everything

www.ketchuponeverything.co.uk
ketchuponeverythingblog.blogspot.co.uk
kay@ketchuponeverything.co.uk

53 // Kay Vincent is originally from the West Midlands in the UK but now lives in London. She studied a degree in Surface Pattern Design at Staffordshire University, and an MA at the Royal College of Art in Printed Textiles. When Kay graduated from university her first experience in London was exhibiting at 'New Designers', where she won two awards. Kay now designs commercially as a freelancer for high street children's clothing brands, and runs her own project, Ketchup on Everything, in her spare time. Her screen-printing is her treat, a more personal journey and a nice break from the fast-paced disposable fashion world. Kay has a passion for rummaging in junk shops for treasures such as retro kids' toys, clothing and books, especially for picture dictionaries which she calls her 'gold'. As her studio name suggests, she also loves eating 'ketchup on everything'. Kay finds being part of Etsy a great inspiration for her work, and also looks to retro design of the 1950s, '60s and '70s and her friend Mark Fox. Her 'bible' whilst at college was Paul Smith's *You Can Find Inspiration in Everything*. In the future Kay would love to create her own children's book that in years to come could become someone else's vintage treasure.

Design Heroes: Paul Smith, Donna Wilson

Favourite Children's Illustrators: John Alcorn, Ingela P. Arrhenius (see pages 144–5), Gloria Kamen

Left / Egg and Soldiers Coasters
Based on Kay's illustration, the coaster set is not only a functional object but also a puzzle that tells a story, according to Kay. A fun way to entertain children at breakfast.

Bottom left / Egg and Soldiers
A five-colour silk screen-print design created in Illustrator combining scanned crayon doodles with very clean computer-generated edges, a contrast look that Kay adores. 'I love the fact that this image has put a smile on so many people's faces when I have done markets,' she says. 'This makes it all worthwhile!' The story goes that the egg stole the moustache of the soldier to his left. That is why the solider looks so embarrassed.

Bottom right / Dandy Lion Screen-Print
Inspired by retro children's learning flash cards, Kay created a quirky, original interpretation of a 'dandy' lion, i.e. a lion who places particular importance upon physical appearance, refined language and leisurely hobbies. Produced in Adobe Illustrator combining Kay's scanned-in crayon doodles with very clean computer-generated edges created in Illustrator. She loves the contrast of her super-messy doodles being constrained by clean edges.

G & SOLDIERS

dandy **LION**

Khristian A. Howell

khristianahowell.com
info@khristianahowell.com

54 // Khristian A. Howell is a designer based in Atlanta, Georgia, in the US. She is renowned for her expertise with colour, pattern and trends. Clients have included Shutterfly, Robert Kaufman Fabrics, REI, Eddie Bauer, Andrews McMeel Publishing, Uncommon and Tiny Prints. In October 2011 Khristian was featured as the 'Woman of Style' in *Better Homes and Gardens* magazine and is now their contributing colour expert. Khristian finds her inspiration in fashion, travel and culture, and hopes her passion for living an inspired life is evident in all her work. In the future Khristian would love to work with CB2, Duralee and The Rug Company.

All designs from The Woodlands Collection by Anthology Fabrics.

Design Heroes: Marimekko (see pages 204–7), Diane von Furstenberg, Florence Broadhurst

Favourite Children's Illustrators: Daniel Chang, Eric Carle

Above / The Woodlands
Detail from the cream colourway of The Woodlands shows the way motifs such as the birds/clouds and little green lollipop trees have been lifted out to create further fabrics in the range.

Top right / Forest
Little fluffy stylized lollipop trees in various shades of green make a wonderful complimentary print for the more pictorial Woodlands design.

Bottom right / Dream
The clouds and birds from the main Woodlands print have been picked out to create a small-scale co-ordinating print in a beautiful shade of turquoise.

Laura Ashley

www.lauraashley.com

55 // Laura Ashley was founded in 1953 by Bernard Ashley, who handled the operational side, and his wife Laura, who was in charge of design. Laura began by printing small squares of fabrics for patchwork, and then moved onto headscarves, placemats and tea towels. By 1967 they were producing 5,000 metres (16,400 feet) of printed fabric per week. It was in the 1980s that they first produced the type of home furnishing collections that we know and love today. They became known for their romantic English style and timeless country house classics. For children's decor the company designs and manufactures everything for the stylish nursery including wallpaper, beds, bedding, cuddly toys, rugs, furniture and more. In 2011 it launched a new girlswear line called 'Laura Ashley Girls' which is described as 'everyday favourites that children remember for a lifetime.'

Top / Clementine Stripe Cotton Fabric
A pretty 100 per cent cotton fabric combining a lovely ditsy floral and gingham design into a single striped print.

Bottom /
Alphabet Wallpaper
A cute and colourful wallpaper that is perfect for both nurseries and children's rooms. The design has a pastel patchwork theme featuring various floral patterns and ginghams. Some of the letters have cute motifs to match each letter and make early learning fun.

Opposite / Woodland Adhesive Wall Stickers
These colourful stickers can be used to decorate walls, books or bedroom furniture. With easy-peel properties, the cute motifs can be used to add interest to plain surfaces.

Opposite /
Woodland Cotton Fabric
A furnishing-quality fabric
that was designed to be
made into curtains and
accessories. The woodland
animals are charming
and pretty without being
overly cute.

Above /
Esme Print Cotton Fabric
A fashionable woodland
theme is given the Laura
Ashley twist by using classic
pastel colours and delicate
pretty motifs such as hearts,
butterflies and polka dots.

Lemon Ribbon

www.lemonribbon.com
info@lemonribbon.com

56 // Melanie Bullock founded Lemon Ribbon in 2009 with Edward Weale. Melanie, Lemon Ribbon's design director, is originally from Hampshire but is now based in London. She studied Fashion Design with Marketing at the University of East London. Melanie's design influences come from a wide range of sources including Swedish and Japanese design, vintage children's illustration, toys and foreign magazines. Being creative for Melanie usually entails a lot of travel or searching the web for inspiration from various sources from which she can take snippets to create something new and original. Inspiration can come from anything – an old toy or postcard, books or museums and antique market stall finds. Lemon Ribbon's clients range from worldwide retailers, suppliers and manufacturers to small independent brands and products. Growing the Lemon Ribbon brand even further is one of their main ambitions. They have had much success in the early years, which has been fantastic, and they will continue to build on it. They would love to explore more possibilities for licensing Lemon Ribbon with other exciting partners and products, to spread their 'little packages of imagination' even further.

Design Heroes: Collier Campbell, Charley Harper, Kate Moross

Favourite Children's Illustrators: Ed Emberley (see pages 104–9), Marc Boutavant (see pages 196–9), Quentin Blake

Top / Lemon Ribbon Badges
A range of contemporary badges designed for spreading the Lemon Ribbon loveliness. They are handed out at trade shows and given to clients as a memorable calling card.

Bottom / Animal Sanctuary Wallpaper
A fresh, contemporary look for little girls' walls. The motifs are arranged in a series of little frames, which is a great device for giving a design structure to this wallpaper pattern. Designed by Lemon Ribbon and licensed by Graham & Brown from the Animal Sanctuary range.

Opposite top / Nostalgic Nursery
The Lemon Ribbon Nursery was created with lots of nostalgic references. Collecting various design motifs together to demonstrate Lemon Ribbon's 'reflective world with a modern twist, creating a perfect playful environment for little ones.'

Opposite bottom / Boys' Toys
Here Melanie has been playing around with some cool boys' toys in the studio's own 'handwriting', bringing a fresh Lemon Ribbon feel to vintage imagery. Perfect for inspiring boys' active imaginations!

totally cosmic starship

75868 FT

SPIKEY!

CoSMIC RoBOT

ROAR

BOY'S TOYS

ROAR

SPEED 56

Lesley Grainger

www.lesleygrainger.com
lesley@lesleygrainger.com

57 // Lesley Grainger is originally from Hull in England but now lives in Orange County, California. Lesley studied for a BA (Hons) degree in Illustration. She is inspired by her faith and her children, as well as colour, nature and animals. In 2008 Lesley started licensing her designs and her whimsical work has caught the eye of some fabulous clients including Target, Happy Spaces, Robert Kaufman and Oopsy Daisy. Lesley's ambition for the future would be to create more children's books.

Design Heroes: Marc Chagall, Paul Klee, Mark Rothko

Favourite Children's Illustrator: Mabel Lucie Atwell

Top / Dinosaurs Rule
Dinosaurs are a perennial favourite for boys' design and decor. Lesley's painterly and fun depiction turns fearsome beasts into friendly characters.

Middle / Flying
Strong lines and earthy colours make this a simple but effective illustration for boys. The subtle background grid adds interest.

Bottom / Racing
This design may be simple in style but it still manages to convey the message of a race track with plenty of colour and movement.

Above / Love Pets
Children will marvel at the variety of animals in this illustration. There is a lot to stimulate a young imagination and the jolly typography adds to the fun mood.

Lisa Martin

lisamartin-illustration.com
lisa-martin-illustration.blogspot.co.uk
hello@lisamartin-illustration.com

58 // Lisa Martin is from Newcastle upon Tyne in the UK but now lives in Leeds, West Yorkshire. Lisa graduated from Leeds College of Art in 2012 with a BA (Hons) in Printed Textiles and Surface Pattern Design. Lisa is inspired by animals, woodland and 'all things bright and quirky!' Lisa creates illustrations and surface pattern designs for the children's market. Eventually she would love to start a print studio in north-east England aimed at new design graduates and focusing on surface pattern design because, she says, 'I'd like to help give new designers a kick-start in their career through freelance work.'

Design Hero: Helen Dardik
(see pages 128–31)

Favourite Children's Illustrator:
Marc Boutavant (see pages 196–9)

Top / Woof Woof
Like the Meow Meow design, this print uses a scattered pattern of cutely drawn faces on a light ground which would be perfect for young babies. Created with children's furnishing fabrics in mind, such as bedding and curtains.

Bottom / Meow Meow
A light and airy design that was created using Adobe Illustrator and hand-drawn textures. Lisa created the polka dot background using inks, then scanned them into Illustrator.

Top / Little Raccoon
Solid colour motifs
really stand out on this
background made from
a scanned-in texture.
Designed during Lisa's
work placement at Lemon
Ribbon, and intended
for children's clothing.

Bottom / Cutesy Squirrel
The graphic line of this cute
squirrel contrasts beautifully
with the more organic lines
of his bushy tail. Created in
Adobe Illustrator, intended
for use on stickers.

Above / Chatterbox
A dapper fox who speaks French and an aloof dog with
an umbrella are just some of the motifs found in Lisa's quirky
designs. Created in Adobe Illustrator using hand-drawn
characters and lots of texture. Intended for children's
furnishing fabrics.

Opposite / Foxy Dancer
This scattered print of a dancing fox has a subtle
hand-drawn texture layered over the top of the motifs
to give depth and add interest. Intended for fabric.

Little Studio

www.littlestudio.se
info@littlestudio.se

59 // Little Studio is the Swedish design team of Angelica Utterberg and Marit Lissdaniels. They are currently based in Karlsborg and Gothenborg, about 32 kilometres (20 miles) apart from each other, but they still do most of their work together via the internet. They mail, discuss and send sketches to each other. They both studied Graphic Design at Hellidens Folkhögskola, Tidaholm, Sweden, which is where the idea for their joint venture was born. They are inspired by many things: what they see, hear, do and what they wear. But a really big inspiration is children and their ability to see things for more than they are. A triangle can be just a triangle, but to a child it can also be a mountain, and simple circles heaped on each other can be soap bubbles. Little Studio have many dreams and ambitions for the future and always set their goals high. They'd like to work on children's clothing and an outdoor collection, but if they dream really big, it would be to design a pattern for Marimekko. Their mission is to make happy design and make people smile.

Design Heroes: Maija Louekari, Sanna Annukka

Favourite Children's Illustrator: Tove Jansson

Opposite / ABC Square
Here a classic serif font
in white really stands out
against the multicoloured
squares. The design is
gender neutral and would
appeal as much to adults
choosing colourful and
stylish decor as it does
to children.

Left / 123 Square
A striking and colourful
printed poster for a
children's room that is both
educational and beautiful.
Marit and Angelica work
with both digital and
hand-drawn techniques,
but for this occasion they
wanted a clean-lined, digital
graphic effect.

Bottom / Apple ABC
The alphabet is always a
popular subject matter for
designers, particularly those
with a passion for graphics
and typography. Here Marit
and Angelica have come up
with a colourful and original
interpretation.

Liz Alpass

theinkhouse.blogspot.com.au
www.etsy.com/shop/TheInkHouse
liz@theinkhouse.com.au

60 // Liz Alpass and her studio label 'The Ink House' are based in Melbourne, Australia, where Liz studied Graphic Design at Swinburne University of Technology. For several years Liz has been designing for a busy greeting, gift and stationery company, but since having her first baby she has been freelancing and dabbling in her own creative pursuits. Liz loves illustrating, crafting, sewing, decorating and being a mum to her beautiful baby girl. For inspiration Liz looks to Japanese culture, colours, unusual houses, oddities, creative blogs, books with great pictures, fables, fabrics, vintage finds such as toys from the past, and her artistic friends. Liz would love to design fabrics, bed linen for kids and other home decor products. Her previous clients have included Target, Big W, Kmart and Woolworths. In the future Liz looks forward to expanding the range of products for her 'The Ink House' brand.

Design Heroes: Matte Stephens, Kukula, Johnny Yanok

Favourite Children's Illustrators: Alice and Martin Provensen, Mary Blair

My Little Vintage Girl

Happy days
of fall

Left / My Little Vintage Girl
This sweet little girl with
a handful of balloons was
created digitally using
Adobe Illustrator with
fills made from scanned
vintage-inspired fabrics.
Part of a collection of prints
for sale in Liz's Etsy shop.

Above / Happy Days of Fall
Giving the impression
of a paper and fabric
collage, this design features
a leafy autumn tree with
falling tangerines and little
singing birds. The orange,
brown and yellow colour
combinations have been
used for a retro twist.

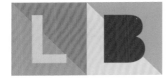

Luli Bunny

www.lulibunny.com
www.ponponbunnies.com.ar
info@lulibunny.com

61 // Luli Bunny is an illustrator and character designer from Buenos Aires, Argentina. She is known for her happy, colourful, cute kawaii-style designs, which often feature bunnies, bears, rodents and other adorable characters. Luli is inspired by vintage illustrations, toys, daily life and small creatures. Her past clients have included Momiji, Philips Avent, La Lectoría, Ivy Press and TweetWorld Application. Luli has exhibited at Puma Urban Art and at Inspiration Fest. Going forward, Luli would love to be able to design more toys because it is so nice to see the characters she has created come to life in 3D.

Design Heroes: Helen Dardik (see pages 128–31), Ingela P. Arrhenius (see pages 144–5), Meomi

Favourite Children's Illustrators: Beatrix Potter, Leo Timmers, Mary Blair

Top / The Golden Age
A personal work featuring a happy elephant riding in a car that was inspired by vintage illustrations and a Beck song.

Bottom / Booglet
Booglet is a little character who wears a frog costume. Luli has chosen to illustrate him with a rainbow frame and snail on his head. This was a commissioned illustration based on a character created by Blackmago. Booglet character © Blackmago.

Top / Vamos a Aprender
(meaning 'We are going to learn' in Spanish)
A cover illustration for a school book featuring two jolly children
learning their letters and numbers. Created for La Lectoria.

Bottom / Rainbow Bunny Pattern
A pattern created for Luli's personal portfolio featuring her
favourite inspiration: bunnies. Used as a background pattern
for her website. Created from scanned-in sketches.

made with love
by mrs booth

www.mrsbooth.com
mrsbooth@mrsbooth.com

62 // Judith Booth is originally from Edinburgh, and recently returned to North Berwick, Scotland, after 20 years living and working in London. She studied for a BA (Hons) in Graphic Design and Communication, at the Duncan of Jordanstone College of Art and Design, in Dundee. Previously Judith worked as a graphic designer at several London design studios and branding agencies, working with clients such as Boots, Marks & Spencer, Laura Ashley and British Airways. She started designing her own range called 'made with love by mrs booth' when she was unable to find the simple, colourful and uncomplicated pictures and colouring books that she remembered from her own childhood for her children. Judith finds inspiration from children's book illustration, packaging and textiles from the '60s and '70s, as well as from her own childhood memories. In the future Judith would love to create her own range of children's books. Judith hopes she has managed to create 'a brand that stays with you – that will become part of the fabric of your childhood.'

Design Heroes: Abram Games, Bob Gill, Charley Harper

Favourite Children's Illustrator: Paul Rand

Opposite top /
Personalized Alphabet Fox
An A4 digital print inspired
by Judith's alphabet frieze.
A stylised fox is curled up
in a ball illustrated with
solid colour and sharp black
outline. Personalization can
be added at the top of every
print to match the animal
and letter of the alphabet.

Opposite bottom /
Personalized Alphabet
Tortoise
Evidence of Judith's love
for '60s and '70s design
can be seen in this retro-
style tortoise illustration.
Like all the designs featured,
it was created for Judith's
own label 'made with love
by mrs booth'. Designed
as an A4 digital print.

Above / Fancy Letters and
Numbers Wrapping Paper
Created for Judith's own
label 'made with love by
mrs booth'. Featuring a
fabulously colourful mix of
tightly packed letters and
numbers, the artwork was
created digitally then litho-
printed onto recycled paper.

Mamas & Papas

www.mamasandpapas.com

63 // Mamas & Papas was founded in 1981 by David and Luisa Scacchetti who were inspired by the birth of their first daughter. They looked to their Italian roots, to a culture bursting with passion, style and elegance to find beautiful, individual things for their baby daughter. Now, over three decades on, and with daughters Amanda and Olivia in the business, Mamas & Papas continues to be at the heart of every parent's journey. Their 60-strong design team take inspiration from a diverse range of sources including fashion, interiors, printmaking and general social and media trends. Innovators within their field, Mamas & Papas prides itself on considered design that successfully encapsulates the height of function with a strong individual design aesthetic, to provide parents with nursery products that offer the highest level of quality, attention to detail and individuality.

Top / Rosie & Rex Bedding by Victoria Ockwell
A print and embroidered bedding collection featuring a woodland landscape of falling leaves and playful characters.

Bottom / Jamboree Canvas by Victoria Ockwell
Hand embroidered and appliquéd canvas using a variety of geometric prints and buttons.

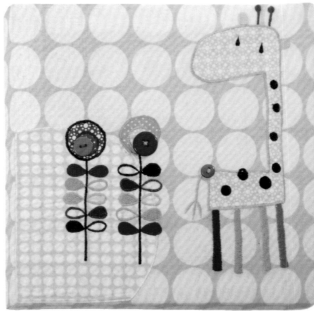

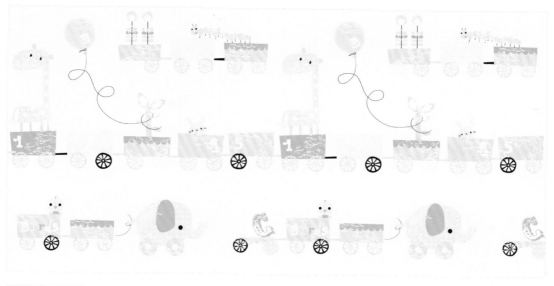

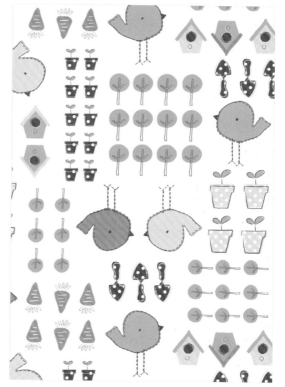

Top / Jamboree Wallpaper by Victoria Ockwell
Part of the Jamboree bedding collection, this bright, fun range is inspired by a circus parade.

Bottom left / Jumble Jungle by Jennifer Chamberlain
A multifunctional pattern, graphic in style, containing cheery, crisp characters and typography with bold primary colours arranged on grid paper. A purposeful and practical print created in Adobe Illustrator.

Bottom right / Garden Patch by Jennifer Chamberlain
Little hopping birdies and clusters of garden-patch motifs are presented in soft muted colours with a hand-drawn feel. This bright, generic pattern was created in Adobe Illustrator.

Opposite / Flora by Dee Leonard
A modern twist on a floral print, with naive childlike floral shapes repeated using a sophisticated yet girly palette. This pattern was created as part of the SS12 Sola pushchair collection and generated in Adobe Illustrator.

Above / Zoo Time by Dee Leonard
Silhouettes of animals tessellating to create a multidirectional repeat pattern with a quirky colour palette. The print was created using Adobe Illustrator for the SS12 Trek buggy collection.

Marc Boutavant

www.heartagency.com/artist/
MarcBoutavant/gallery/1
marc.boutavant@wanadoo.fr

64 // Marc Boutavant is a French graphic artist, illustrator and writer. Originally from Burgundy, Marc now lives in Paris where he spent two years studying visual communication. Marc works largely on children's books but also illustrates for children's products with companies such as Atomic Soda, Petit Jour, Djeco and Blue Q. Marc's main inspiration is childhood, first from memories of his own, and now from watching his children. It is not only his children's behaviour that inspires him but also the memories they pull up from his own past. If he could choose a dream design commission it would be to create 'crazy children's furniture'. Marc plans to continue writing and illustrating children's books and to create characters that will hopefully inspire more animation projects.

Design Heroes: Sonia Delaunay, Dick Bruna, Javier Mariscal

Favourite Children's Illustrators: Fabio Viscogliosi, Anouk Ricard, Emile Bravo

Top / Children's Books
Using a limited colour palette here gives Marc's work a nostalgic feel. The handwritten script is the perfect accompaniment to the whimsical characters. As with most of Marc's work, the more you look, the more you will see. Created for a feature on children's books for *The New York Times* supplement in 2008.

Bottom / *For Just One Day*, Cover
The cover design for the 2009 book *For Just One Day* written by Laura Leuck and illustrated by Marc. The bright yellow background and bold typography really make this cover stand out on the bookshelf. Published by Chronicle Books.

Top left / Porcupine
A page from *For Just One Day*. The book is designed as a guessing game where the answer is revealed over the next page. Here a charming porcupine reclining in a cactus has his needles combed and decorated with flowers.

Top right / Snake
A page from the book *For Just One Day*. A vivacious illustration full of humour and wit. A friendly, smiling snake uses his rattle to create music for cute dancing rats. Marc has the amazing ability to make his animals come alive with personality.

Left / Endings
Another page from the book *For Just One Day*. The books ends with a gallery of all the children encountered throughout the book. Marc has created a superb variety of children's faces, hairstyles and frames.

Opposite / Overnighter Bag
This incredible illustration was used on a bag by BlueQ in 2010. Bursting with animal characters and detail, there is so 'much to see in every part of this design. One of the devices Marc uses to create his heart-warming characters is human-like expressions and large eyes that connect with the viewer.

Above / MultiMouk
Mouk is an adorable and intrepid little bear who has become enormously popular through the wonderful illustrations and stories in Marc's books. Mouk also has his own animated television series produced by the French company Millimages. This pattern featuring various Mouk images in repeat has lots of different scenes to explore and was created for use on various licensed Mouk products.

Margo Slingerland

www.margoslingerland.nl
www.gosi-land.com
info@margoslingerland.nl

65 // Margo Slingerland is based in Amsterdam in the Netherlands. She graduated at the Design Academy Eindhoven in 2004. Before Margo started her own design studio, she worked for famous Dutch brands Oilily and gsus sindustries. Besides working on her own collections, Margo also works as a freelancer for all kinds of clients including fashion brands and supermarket chains. Her inspiration comes from all over: flea markets, children's books and movies, video clips, fabric shops, nice people, etc. Children inspire her, and her own childhood is also a source of inspiration. Margo's dream for the future is to spend all her time on her own design projects without making (too many) concessions.

Design Heroes: Yoshitomo Nara, Tim Walker

Favourite Children's Illustrator: Fiep Westendorp

Top / Sweethearts and Bows Wrapping Paper
Bottom / Sweethearts and Bows Badges
For this collection Margo mixed different techniques. She loves to combine 2D with 3D, old with new, sweet with tough, colourful with black and white. The wrapping paper and badges were developed in collaboration with a Dutch company, Kado Design, who asked Margo to design a 'special edition' collection for them.

Top left / GOSI Postcard, Hello Girl

Top right / GOSI Postcard, Congratulations Girl
For these postcards Margo used different techniques.
She combined hand drawings with 3D made elements
which she photographed. She also made little patterns
in Illustrator for the backgrounds. The postcards are
made for her collection GOSI.

Bottom left / Sweethearts and Bows Deer in Love Notebook

Bottom right / Sweethearts and Bows Blue Birds Notebook

Marie Perkins

www.inkjet-designs.com
inkjetdesigns.blogspot.co.uk
inkjetdesigns@hotmail.co.uk

66 // Marie Perkins studied Graphic Design and Illustration at Salisbury College of Art in the UK before moving to Brighton to paint pottery. She began working as an in-house textile designer in 2001, creating prints for clients such as Marks & Spencer, Asda, BHS and Homebase. In 2006 she started the Print & Pattern blog to raise awareness of the world of surface pattern design. Now working as a freelance designer, Marie creates designs for greetings cards, wrapping paper, fabrics and more. Clients have included Paperchase, Joseph Joseph, Robert Kaufman and Cardmix. Marie's dream ambition would be to have her studio and work featured in an Édition Paumes book.

Design Heroes: Cath Kidston (see pages 72-7), Orla Kiely (see pages 232-3), Tricia Guild (see pages 98-9)

Favourite Children's Illustrators: Alain Grée (see pages 10-15), Marc Boutavant (see pages 196-9), Hergé

Top / Cars
Little retro cars have been given a folksy Scandinavian feel. Created in Adobe Illustrator with a view to using them for children's wall art, wallpaper or fabrics.

Bottom / Circus Cards
Two birthday card designs which came out of a whole series of circus designs. Brightly coloured balloons and bunting add to the party feel.

Opposite / Roar
The image of a lion has been pared down to simple geometric forms to create this bold repeat pattern. The aim was to create a Scandinavian feel that is both fresh and colourful. The design is part of a collection and has been licensed to Robert Kaufman for use on fabric.

Marimekko

www.marimekko.com
info@marimekko.fi

67 // Marimekko is a fabric company well-known for their bold patterns and organic designs. It was founded in Finland in 1951 by Armi and Viljo Ratia. The name Marimekko was chosen as it contains an anagram of Armi and 'mekko', the Finnish word for 'dress'. They began as textile producers but branched out into clothing as a way of showing how the fabrics could be used. In 1964 Maija Isola created probably their most famous design, Unikko, which is still in production today. Their colourful design style, characterized by simplicity, clean lines and bright colours, was clearly suited to children's design. Soon Marimekko had developed children's fabrics and bedlinen, and now, under the header 'Tykes Turf', they produce bibs, towels, tableware and accessories.

Right / Bo Boo
This colourful children's print was designed by Japanese artist Katsuji Wakisaka in 1975 and has since gone on to become a classic. The pattern is filled with cars, lorries, buses and pick-up trucks in primary colours and simple shapes, which have a timeless appeal.

Opposite /
Merimerkit (Sea Marks) Designed by Jenni Tuominen in 2011. A striking geometric print, again with a nautical flavour, that will co-ordinate perfectly with Laivakoira (overleaf).

Mélusine Allirol

melusine-allirol.blogspot.fr
allirolmelusine@yahoo.fr

68 // Mélusine Allirol was born in Lyon, France, and lived for a long time in the south of France. She studied at Emile Cohl, an art school in Lyon. Mélusine now lives and works in Strasbourg where she shares a workshop with several other illustrators in an attractive district of the city. Mélusine designs textile objects, illustrations, children's books and toys. She was inspired by the arrival of her little boy, named César, to create children's toys and books. Her series of books *Les Petites Découvertes de César et Rose*, published by Editions Lito, are named after him.

Design Heroes: Shinzi Katoh, ferm LIVING (see pages 116–9), Lalé

Favourite Children's Illustrators: Richard Scarry, Gyo Fujikawa, Nami Adachi

Top / Funny Cushion Covers
The unifying element in all of these designs is the way Mélusine has illustrated the eyes. Combined with the little smiles, they make a cute and appealing collection. Printed and sold by Envelop.

Bottom / Basile
Timeless classic toys never go out of style, like this charming dog designed by Mélusine as a wooden pull-along toy. Designed for Vilac.

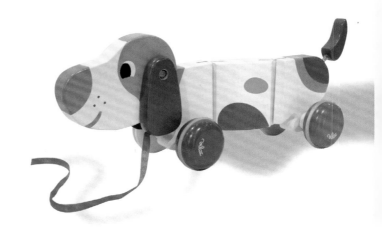

Top / The Coloured Rain
A parade of cute characters walk beneath colourful rain clouds on this puzzle designed for Vilac.

Middle / The Cute Race
Smiling animals whizz past in fast cars on this puzzle designed for Vilac.

Bottom /
Mister and Miss Bear
Two adorable bears feature on posters designed for the renowned art website L'Affiche Moderne.
en.laffichemoderne.com

Michéle Brummer Everett

mlbeverett.com
mlbe.tumblr.com
michele@mlbeverett.com

69 // Michéle Brummer Everett is originally from South Africa but is now based in the US. Michéle received her degree from The School of the Art Institute of Chicago where she focused mainly on drawing, printmaking and textile design. Her most recent clients have been Cloud 9 Fabrics, Sycamore Street Press and *Georges* magazine. Michéle finds inspiration in natural history museums, Roald Dahl books, the *Uncle* series by J.P. Martin and artwork done by children. In the future Michéle would love to write and illustrate her own books, have her own line of Post-it notes and stickers, illustrate a board game and design museum displays for children.

Design Heroes: Lab Partners, Millimeter Milligram, Tad Carpenter

Favourite Children's Illustrators: Carson Ellis, Taro Gomi, Sol Linero

Top / Redguy
The black lines, simple forms and primary colours give this charming image a retro feel echoing children's books of the 1960s and '70s. This character is so simple, yet you can't help but be captivated by his style.

Bottom / Mushrooms
The shapes of these mushrooms are lightly drawn at the stem and filled with a beautiful, complimentary palette of solid colours at the top making a simple but very striking design.

HOMETOWN

Top / Hulatime
Michéle is not afraid to use unusual colour palettes, which make her work more distinctive. Here three little sketchy girls in vivid hues look fabulous against the grey background.

Bottom / Hometown
All of Michéle's designs featured were created in Adobe Illustrator. The images were hand-drawn using a Wacom tablet, enabling Michéle to draw straight onto the screen. Here she has used very simple forms for the houses and sketch-like doodles over the top to add detail.

Overleaf / Monsterz
These cute little characters are made by using basic shapes of flat colour and adding dots, lines and other minimal marks over the top in a pencil line effect. These provide all of the details needed to illustrate the monsterz, including faces, arms, legs, spectacles, etc. Design for a children's fabric line by Cloud 9 Fabrics.

minimega

www.minimegadesign.dk
www.minimegadesign.dk/blog

70 // minimega is the design studio of Sara Andersen, based in Aarhus, Denmark. Sara studied Graphic Design at the Hojer Design College in Denmark and now works for a number of Danish clients. Sara finds her inspiration from travels, magazines, Japanese books (interior and origami), her children's toys, flea markets, shop windows, cute packaging designs and the 'wonderful internet'. Sara is also a collector of bits and bobs – especially pretty paper, but also colourful beads, Japanese masking tapes, straws, strings etc. All of these little things inspire her too and put her in a creative mood. Her dream commission would be to design a collection of really nice, exclusive origami paper, or crazy packaging design for children's sweets. Sara currently works from a studio at her home, which is perfect at the moment with two small children, but in the future she hopes to set up a shared studio in the middle of Aarhus.

Design Heroes: Lili Scratchy, Rob Lowe (Supermundane), Fernando Volken Togni

Favourite Children's Illustrators: Anders Arhoj, Elisabeth Dunker, Ingela P. Arrhenius (see pages 144–5)

Top / Cat Card
Bottom / Mouse Card
Sara has a love for graphic clarity and clean lines. Here she has pared the natural shapes of a cat and mouse down to their simplest form. Before she opens her Mac, Sara always starts her illustrations with a quick pen sketch to figure out colours and dimensions. She then draws the design in Adobe Illustrator using a Wacom pen. Created for minimega greetings cards.

Opposite top / Cat and Mouse Posters
The cat and mouse posters have a bolder look with solid coloured backgrounds and a sans serif bubble-style font. The cheeky wink adds a touch of whimsy.

Opposite bottom /
Whale and Lion Posters
A selection of minimega products including greetings cards, wrapping paper and children's posters. A whale and a lion feature on these educational prints featuring letters and numbers in a classic serif font on white.

Mondaland

www.mondaland.co.uk
www.mondaland.carbonmade.com
studio@mondaland.co.uk

71 // Vanessa Waller of Mondaland is based in Berkshire, UK. She graduated in 1998 with a degree in Design Crafts from Cumbria College of Art and Design, where she specialized in printed and multi-media textiles. Vanessa worked in various non-design related jobs for the following 12 years, but in 2010 she decided to leave her job and follow her dream, and with savings in hand she took herself on a 'zero to hero' Adobe Illustrator course; in a week she had learnt the basics of Illustrator. Vanessa then started to build her portfolio and work for herself as a designer/maker. She sells her design work, fabric, soft toys and art prints via online shops including Not on the High Street, Etsy, Spoonflower and Society6. Clients have included Tigerprint Studios (for Marks & Spencer). Vanessa loves the bold graphic patterns that were synonymous with the 1960s and '70s. The era's bright colour palettes, strong motifs and offset screen-prints particularly appeal. She is also inspired by children's book illustration and has very fond memories of picture books from her childhood. Also, since becoming pregnant with her first baby she has been massively inspired by the wealth of eye-catching designs for babies and children. She has no doubt that this is having an influence on her design work too.

Design Heroes: Angie Lewin, Helen Dardik (see pages 128–31), Jane Ormes

Favourite Children's Illustrators: Oliver Jeffers, Judith Kerr, Marc Boutavant (see pages 196–9)

Above / Geomog
These block-colour cats have slightly sharp, angular edges which are contrasted perfectly with the loose linework that gives them their features.

Opposite top / Rootin Tootin
A novelty print with a grow-your-own-vegetables theme. The vegetables have been anthropomorphized with faces to encourage children to connect with them as characters.

Bottom left / Baby Bear
Sketchy linework on these baby bears gives them a hand-drawn look. The colours are warm, stylish and sophisticated. The pink background grid provides all-over interest. Vanessa's designs nearly always start as pencil drawings in her sketchbook. Once she is happy with a hand-drawn design/element she'll then redraw it in Adobe Illustrator.

Bottom right / Autumn Forest
Owls are a popular motif for children's design thanks to their association with wisdom and learning. Vanessa has used crosshatch and graphic circles to give this pattern a very modern feel.

My Lovely Spot

www.mylovelyspot.de
wibke@mylovelyspot.de

72 // Wibke Kruse has run her own little label, My Lovely Spot, since 2008 in Hamburg, Germany. Wibke studied Fashion Design at Hanover's University of Applied Sciences and Art and now works as a freelance textile designer. For My Lovely Spot, Wibke loves to design funny and colourful characters that you can't help but become fond of. She is inspired by well-shaped, timeless, modern design, as well as works from the 1960s and '70s. She loves a mix of old and new styles and techniques, and finds ideas in old books from flea markets and memories of her own childhood. Wibke believes design should be fun for all ages and her two children are her most important critics.

Favourite Children's Illustrators:
Alain Grée (see pages 10-15),
Ed Emberley (see pages 104-9),
Fiep Westendorp, Miroslav Sasek

Top / Lovelyspot
A winding road leads the eye to an owl and a rainbow in this T-shirt design for children.

Bottom / Wildlife
An animal print designed for wrapping paper is given a very colourful look with bright flowers, spots and rainbows.

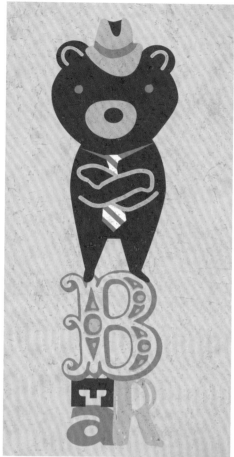

Top left / Pony
This friendly white adorned pony really stands out against the textured background. Created as a postcard for My Lovely Spot using a combination of vector and tablet-based hand-drawing technique.

Top right / Bear
Wibke likes working on vector-based drawings in Adobe Illustrator, followed up and combined with hand-drawn or scanned material in Adobe Photoshop. Here she has created a design for a poster featuring a smart-looking bear in a hat and tie, standing on top of some fabulous typography.

Bottom / We Love Music
Three super-cool animals with arms crossed listen to a record in this design for the My Lovely Spot postcard series.

Nancy Wolff

www.nancywolff.com
www.loboloup.com
nancy@nancywolff.com

73 //   Nancy Wolff grew up in New Jersey but moved to New York City after studying Fine Art at Skidmore College. Nancy has designed for clients such as Galison, Great Arrow Graphics, Kokka, Nickelodeon, Oopsy Daisy and Unicef. She has also authored and illustrated several children's books published by Henry Holt. It was the covers of *The New Yorker* magazine, Saul Steinberg's in particular, that first clued Wendy into the idea that illustration could possibly be a career choice. In 2012 Nancy and her niece Elizabeth Wolff started a company, Loboloup, specializing in contemporary wallpaper for kids. Loboloup's signature is fresh, innovative illustrations and typography, and a commitment to creating child- and eco-friendly products. Their designs are conceived and painted by hand, then hand silk-screened locally in the US in small batches using water-based inks and organic paper. Nancy's ambition is to paper all the dingy, boring and uncared for walls, in all the kids' bedrooms, throughout the land.

Design Heroes: Saul Steinberg, Sonia Delaunay, Alexander Girard

Favourite Children's Illustrators: Maira Kalman, Oliver Jeffers, Abner Graboff

Opposite / The Big Top
All the fun of the circus is found in this jolly design which Nancy hand-painted with gouache. The warm reds, oranges and yellows look great when set against the neutral grey background. It was created for wallpaper for Muffin and Mani, Australia, and for fabric with Kokka, Japan.

Top / Into the Wild
A fun forest print that has a lovely balance between the solid and the linear. The use of dotty patterns on wings, tails and trees adds detail. Hand-painted with gouache and created for wallpaper for Muffin and Mani, Australia.

Bottom /
A Herd of Patterned Elephants
These cheerful elephants were hand-painted with gouache and feature painterly patterns and pieces of newsprint. Created for wallpaper for Muffin and Mani, Australia, and modified for Kokka, Japan on fabric.

Nina van de Goor

ninainvorm.punt.nl
ninainvorm.etsy.com
ik_ben_nina@hotmail.com

74 // Dutch artist Nina van de Goor lives in the beautiful historic Netherlands city of Den Bosch. Nina's favourite medium for her artwork is ceramics/dinnerware, and not only does she make her own, but she also takes beautiful mid-century modern vintage ceramics and redecorates them with her own hand screen-printed designs, such as brightly coloured branches and flowers, bunting, birds and typography. Besides working with ceramics Nina also makes collages, screen-prints and cards, which she sells in her Etsy shop. She is inspired by vintage design, illustration and ceramics, and by folklore-inspired and ethnic prints. Beautiful little things in everyday life, like typography or product wrapping, also inspire her. Nina runs the wonderful and popular design blog 'Ninainvorm', a title which roughly translates to mean 'Nina in Shape'. After her daughter was born, Nina focused a lot more on children's design. 'I love making things for her, such as the mural in her room or her own ceramics set,' she says. In the future Nina would love to design tableware in larger quantities. She currently makes one-of-a-kind ceramics, but thinks it would be great to see her work in production.

Design Heroes: Patricia Urquiola, Eva Zeisel, Finn Juhl

Favourite Children's Illustrators: Charley Harper, Fiep Westendorp, Eric Carle

Opposite top / All the Birds
Whilst taking an early screen-printing class Nina first had to make a quick print using scraps of paper, without caring for the design, just to try out the printing technique. But instead of tearing random paper to pieces, Nina couldn't help but quickly cut out a few bird shapes. She then added collaged paper wings and eyes.

Opposite bottom /
A Starry Night for my Baby Girl
This collage, originally created for a birth announcement for the arrival of Nina's baby daughter Rosa, features a variety of papers such as origami, newspaper, and photographs torn from magazines.

Above / Alphabet Print
Lower case letters with a lovely loose look make up this colourful alphabet print. Nina originally cut the letters out of black paper and then coloured them digitally.

Top / Strawberry Nameprint for Maantje Piet
Bottom / Strawberry Nameprint for Rosa Lieve
Nina wanted to create a modern version of the embroidered 'birth samplers'
that many of us had when we were kids: something that's sweet and
personal, but also whimsical, fresh and modern. Her personalized cards
use her recognizable hand-cut letters and demonstrate her love of bold
colours and strong forms.

Top / My Colourful Garden
Made using a colourful collage of brightly coloured papers, this scene features Nina's trademark bunting motifs, which are geometric but cheery. Here they are neatly strung between stylized trees.

Bottom / Washi Tape Mural
Nina made this mural for her daughter Rosa's bedroom mural using only removable Japanese washi masking tapes. Nina had to work with the specific characteristics and limitations of the masking tape and so she chose a design that used straight lines and singular shapes as much as possible.

Noi Publishing

www.noipublishing.com
enquiries@noipublishing.com

75 // Tracy Francis spent her childhood in South Africa, where she also studied Graphic Design on a course that involved lots of life drawing and illustration. Now based in Farnham, in the UK, Tracy runs Noi Publishing, a family firm, with her partner Peter Francis and his twin brother Paul. Tracy worked for a long time in design studios for big clients doing packaging and print design. Tracy believes that being a designer for so long makes you a bit of a magpie, so her design heroes are many and varied. At the moment she is inspired by the big name bloggers who 'sweep up all that is out there and present it to us with our morning cup of coffee'. Her daughters are her biggest critics and have final say. Tracy thinks it is so good for them to be around the creative process and they get very involved. 'They can often draw characters better than I can,' she says. 'They just get down and do it, and get right to the heart of the character in just a few lines.'

Design Heroes: Karin Daymond, Tom Ford, Tricia Guild (see pages 98–9)

Favourite Children's Illustrators: Marcel Marlier, Shirley Hughes, Niki Daly

Top / Kitty Invite
Kittens with oversized heads and sketchy stripes look sweet on this party invitation.

Bottom / Juggling Sheep
An adorable little sheep, whose scribble-like fleece resembles knitting, juggles tiny cakes.

Happy Birthday

Above / Skateboarding Fox
A real sense of movement from the tilted skateboard and irregular type can be seen in this joyful design. Touches of scribble give it a hand-drawn feel.

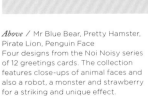

Above / Mr Blue Bear, Pretty Hamster, Pirate Lion, Penguin Face
Four designs from the Noi Noisy series of 12 greetings cards. The collection features close-ups of animal faces and also a robot, a monster and strawberry for a striking and unique effect.

Opposite / Little Girl 1, Little Boy 1, Pirate Croc, Smart Soldier
Four cards from the Noi Kids range of birthday greetings cards. The range includes 18 cards, including some especially for ages one to three with motifs for boys and girls, all in a vibrant, loosely illustrated style.

Happy Birthday

Happy Birthday

Orla Kiely

www.orlakiely.com
www.egmont.co.uk

76 // Orla Kiely is an Irish designer based in London. Orla originally studied Textile Design in Dublin and later took a Masters degree at the Royal College of Art in London. In 1995 Orla Kiely set up her own label creating fashion accessories. She is renowned for her designs, which have an emphasis on graphic pattern and colour. Her signature stem print has become a recognizable branded image all around the world. Orla has a love of mid-century design and this influence is evident in her prints. Orla Kiely now produces not only fashion and accessory collections but also bedlinen, stationery, wallpaper, ceramics, radios and even a car. In 2011 Orla was awarded an honorary OBE in recognition of her services to business and the fashion industry, making her one of the UK's most eminent designers. In 2011 she collaborated with Egmont publishers to produce several board books for very young children using her bold, colourful graphic style.

Design Heroes: André Courrèges, Arne Jacobsen, Finn Juhl

Favourite Children's Illustrators: Paul Rand, Dick Bruna, Saul Bass

Above / Colours, Numbers covers Copyright © 2011 Orla Kiely. Published by Egmont UK Ltd and used with permission.
The covers of Orla Kiely's children's books feature her iconic stem print overlaid with a band of colourful type. Each book in the series is given a different background colour, with the design layout remaining the same to create a co-ordinating set. Their quality is deliberately high spec in keeping with the style of Orla's own products, and they feature woven fabric-textured covers and extra heavyweight board. The eye-catching colourful design really makes them stand out from other baby books on the shelf.

Opposite /
One House, Two Apples, Ten Cars From *Numbers.* Copyright © 2011 Orla Kiely. Published by Egmont UK Ltd and used with permission.
Three double pages from Orla Kiely's book show how her simple graphic style can work perfectly for babies whilst still being incredibly sophisticated. The colour palette is typically Orla, rather than using conventional colours associated with baby's books. Taking the theme of simple counting from one to ten, Orla has pared the various motifs down to simple, clean-lined graphic forms but has also added clever background pattern detailing and a stylish font for the numbers.

 **one**

 **two**

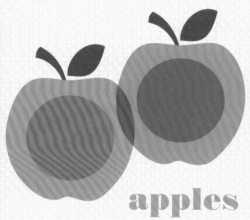 **apples**

 **ten**

 cars

PaaPii Design

paapiidesign.com
paapii-blogi.blogspot.com
info@paapiidesign.com

77 //   Anniina Isokangas is the designer and mother of two behind PaaPii Design, based in Kokkola, Finland. Anniina graduated from Kuopio Academy of Design in 2004 with a BA in Ceramics and Glass Design and now runs her own children's textile design and manufacturing company. She loves bright coloured retro/Scandinavian-style fabrics and a lot of her influences come from vintage children's books. Anniina designs hand-printed fabric soft toys and do-it-yourself sewing kits, along with other textiles such as children's bedlinen and clothes. She hand screen-prints the fabrics herself and all of PaaPii's products are Oeko-Tex compliant (free from harmful substance), which is important when designing products for children. Anniina has grown her business from her kitchen table to having stockists all over the world. In the future she really would like to see some of her bedlinen designs go into production. Her heart is in children's design and she hopes that it will be possible to continue in this area.

Design Heroes: Maija Louekari, Kaj Franck, Maija Isola

Favourite Children's Illustrators: Camilla Mickwitz, Tove Jansson, Zdeněk Miler

Opposite top /
Leijonat lakanat (Lion Sheets)
Designed for children's
bedlinen the Lion pattern was
made in four different one-
colour prints to suit all tastes:
red, green, blue and yellow.

Opposite bottom /
Kultaleijona (Golden Lion)
This beautiful lion motif
captures the essence
of Scandinavian design –
bold in style and colour
and yet delightfully simple.

Above / Leijonat (Lions)
In the repeat pattern the
lion motifs jigsaw together
perfectly when every other
row is rotated.

Left / Bambi
This little soft toy is one of
PaaPii's best selling products.
Anniina sells them ready made
or as a kit for the customer
to make themselves.

Paper Moon

www.hellopapermoon.co.uk
info@hellopapermoon.co.uk

78 // Nicola Davidson of Paper Moon grew up in the Sussex countryside but is currently based in south London. She studied for a Decorative Arts degree at Nottingham Trent University, specializing in screen-printed textiles. This opened up a whole new world for Nicola, with the endless possibilities that pattern design and illustration can offer. Nicola has designed for a range of retailers and publishing houses in the UK and internationally on both an in-house and freelance basis. She has designed prints for stationery, childrenswear, cards, wrapping paper, tablewares and accessories. Nicola is inspired by beautifully illustrated children's books, nature, travel to new and exciting places, 1950s Scandinavian design, folk art, vintage textiles and ceramics, and architecture. In the future Nicola would love to write and illustrate a children's book and have her own range of children's products.

Design Heroes: Lucienne Day, Olle Eksell, Stig Lindberg

Favourite Children's Illustrators: Miroslav Sasek, Oliver Jeffers, Jon Klassen

Left / Meadow Floral
A fabulously fresh floral design featuring mini geometric shapes to form the details of the flower centres. A combination of hand-drawn elements and textured layers were scanned and further developed using Adobe Illustrator. Inspired by walks in the Sussex countryside.

Above / Whimsy Frames
This design brings together all the motifs used in the collection in one unifying print. Whimsical characters that were created using hand drawings in addition to pen and ink for the florals. Coloured using Adobe Illustrator and designed to be an artwork for a bedroom/nursery.

Opposite / Rainy Days and Lollipops
A wonderful scattered motif design
from a collection of children's prints.
Hand-drawn elements were combined
with ink and further developed using
Adobe Illustrator to add colour.
Inspired by rainy London days.

Above / Chatting Chaps
Cute little characters' faces developed
for a greetings card design. Created
using hand drawings combined
with textured paper and coloured
in Adobe Illustrator.

Paperchase

www.paperchase.com

79 // Paperchase are Britain's leading retailers of design-led and innovative stationery, with over 100 outlets in the UK as well as stores in Denmark, Ireland, Holland and the Middle East. In 2010 they launched a new online store. Paperchase have firmly established themselves as the number one destination for new and fashionable design on stationery, cards and gifts. Their colourful and stylish surface designs are constantly changing and the majority of their merchandise is exclusive. Paperchase have an in-house design team and buy artwork from trade shows. They also have established relationships with several design studios. Children love their products; they offer a wide selection of designs aimed at all ages, from baby's first photo album to the latest teenage graphics on a laptop skin. Just some of their fun children's products include school bags, lunch boxes, tableware, cutlery, stickers, notebooks and pencil cases.

Top / Bubble and Sweet Album
Bubble and Sweet is a design that demonstrates something Paperchase always excel in – creating colourful and fun character ranges. This one featured kawaii style creatures who lived in a landscape of rainbows, mushrooms and happy mountains. Shown here on a photograph album, Bubble and Sweet was available across a whole range of products.

Bottom / Spring Scene Organizer
A collection of fashionable little motifs of fruit and flowers mixed with a wise owl feature on this mini mid-year organizer.

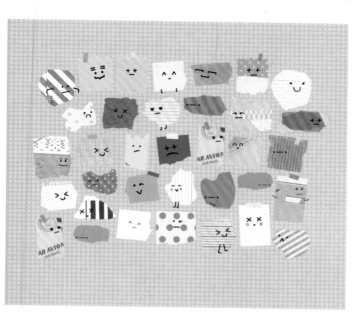

Left / Tearaways
The Tearaways are made from lots of little pieces of torn paper: ruled paper, corrugated paper and even paper from old airmail envelopes. A variety of facial expressions have been drawn on top to bring them to life, and some are held in place with masking tape.

Middle left /
Tearaways A5 notebook
The Tearaways background is made from subtle tone-on-tone blue dots tightly packed together.

Middle right /
Tearaways Overnight Bag
This cute bag in coated canvas is perfect for holidays, school, sports kit or weekends away.

Bottom left / Heads Up
Rows of colourful animals' faces are lined up in this cute print. The edges have the look of being cut out roughly with scissors from coloured paper as there are no curved lines – even on their tiny eyes.

Bottom right /
Heads Up Lunch Bag
Designed to keep a packed lunch cool and fresh. The typeface on the name card has been perfectly chosen to accompany the illustration style.

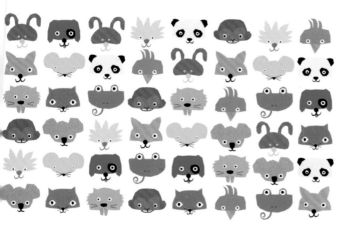

Opposite / Head Chef
A fabulous stylized, graphic pattern that would appeal to all age groups. A selection of chefs, both human and animal, bake and decorate cakes. Devices such as the wavy lines of icing from a piping bag are interesting touches.

Left / Head Chef Recipe File
A decorative file for jotting down and storing recipes will encourage children to take an interest in cooking. With space to write recipes, as well as plastic wallets and pockets.

Below /
Head Chef Snack Boxes
Four of the chef motifs have been lifted out of the main pattern to feature on these stylish lunch boxes. The sharp, clean lines and colours have a vintage storybook quality.

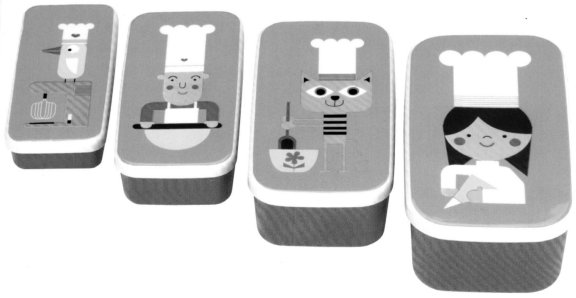

Paulita Ortiz

paulitaortiz.blogspot.com
paulitaortiz@yahoo.com

80 // Paulita Ortiz is originally from Medellín, Colombia, where she studied Graphic Design at the Corporación Colegiatura Colombiana. Now based in Buenos Aires, Argentina, Paulita likes to approach her design work in an intuitive way, especially when it comes to colour. She is inspired by the delicacy of plants and by children's books. Paulita says there are memories of her childhood that are still influential, such as games, animals and insects. In the future Paulita would like to design toys. She enjoys a lot of hand sketching in illustration, and combining her illustrations with patterns to develop prints for products.

Design Heroes: Nate Williams, Helen Dardik (see pages 128–31), Stuart Kolakovic

Favourite Children's Illustrator: Isidro Ferrer

Top / Fantasy
© www.offcorss.com
This cute little baby pattern, featuring a lovely light alphabet print, was used on pyjamas for 0 to 12 month olds. Paulita began the process with a series of sketches, then scanned them into Adobe Illustrator.

Bottom / Creeper Flowers
© www.offcorss.com
This bold floral striped pattern was created digitally, working first in Adobe Photoshop and then Adobe Illustrator. Designed for babies' garments.

Opposite / Forest Friends
© www.offcorss.com
Paulita sketched all the elements of this design separately and then composed the layout and colour in Adobe Illustrator. This pattern was used on pyjamas for babies from 0 to 12 months.

day in the forest

Pepillo

www.pepillo.fr
www.plicplocwiz.com
celine@pepillo.fr

81 // Céline Vernier is the designer behind Pepillo. Originally from northern France, Céline is currently based in Paris. She studied at the Ecole des Beaux-Arts de Tourcoing. Besides her own brand Pepillo, Céline has also designed for L'Affiche Moderne and Lilipinso. Céline's influences and inspirations come from building blocks, 1950s furniture, Ray and Charles Eames, Paul Cox and Katsumi Komagata, as well as spring and bright colours like red, yellow and blue. Of course Céline's children have also been a big influence; she has bought books, toys, building blocks and stickers for them, and has been completely seduced by these objects and the way children perceive them. For the future, Céline would like to carry on designing creative games (real and digital ones), but she would also like to design homewares such as tableware or linen.

Design Heroes: Bruno Munari, Paul Cox, Tom van der Bruggen

Favourite Children's Illustrators: Blexbolex, Lili Scratchy, Alain Grée (see pages 10–15)

Top / A Gift for You (Apple) This design demonstrates Céline's skill at creating strong, playful graphic motifs. This was originally created as a tribute to the late visionary Steve Jobs.

Bottom / Le Chat de Noël Geometric forms depict a cat and a house in this distilled and uncluttered design. Created by Céline for her children with her application Plic, Ploc, Wiz.

Top / Balade à Paris
This limited edition decorative poster, featuring Paris as if it were made from children's building blocks, was created for renowned art publishers L'Affiche Moderne.

Bottom left / Les Amis
A limited edition decorative poster created for L'Affiche Moderne. On these little characters the small eyes, mouths and legs were all hand-drawn and then reworked in Adobe Illustrator.

Bottom right / La Ville d'Anatole
This illustration was created by a 5-year-old called Anatole using the Pepillo iPad and iPhone application Céline designed, called Plic, Ploc, Wiz. It allows children to arrange and play with shapes.

Pink Light Design

www.pinklightdesign.com
pinkhappythoughtsalways.blogspot.com
marybeth@pinklightdesign.com

82 // Pink Light Design is based in Seattle, Washington state, in the US. Its Creative Director is Mary Beth Freet, who is originally from a small town in Washington state. Mary Beth received a Bachelor of Fine Arts degree in Visual Communication from the University of Washington. Before founding Pink Light, Mary Beth worked at Nordstrom for eight years designing textile artwork for their childrenswear line. She also worked for a well-known fashion design studio based in New York, and her artwork has sold to major children's retailers around the world. Her clients have included Class Act Stationery and Accessories, Pier 1 Imports, Scholastic Books, Design Design, Robert Kaufman and Oopsy Daisy. Mary Beth is influenced mostly by creating designs that will make people happy and feel good. She is inspired by nature and fashion, and looks to the past for ways to update traditional design elements to make them fresh, modern and fun. Her ambition for the future would be to design a complete childrenswear line, and children's bedding, lamps, wall art and rugs all under her Pink Light or Pink Chandelier label.

Design Heroes: Kelly Wearstler, Florence Broadhurst, Lilly Pulitzer

Favourite Children's Illustrator: Shel Silverstein

Above / Giggle
A motivational typographic design which was licensed to Oopsy Daisy. The type was created in Adobe Illustrator with the texture added in Photoshop.

Opposite top / A Gift for You
Dark backgrounds can work for children's design when they are mixed with a palette of bold, bright colours, as they are here in Mary Beth's design featuring little creatures delivering presents. Created in Adobe Illustrator with various products in mind.

Opposite bottom left / Shine
A cheerful explosion of colour has been created in this design, which was produced with a variety of end products in mind. The colours, motifs and message are full of joy and could be used for greetings cards, wall art, etc.

Opposite bottom right / Bird Song
A rainbow-bright tree with a singing bird sits in a landscape of multicoloured hills. Everything is outlined in a thick white border to separate it from the blue sky. Created in Adobe Illustrator with a variety of products in mind such as greetings cards, notebooks, fabric, wall art and notebooks.

YOU
are my sunshine
thank you for
shining your
light on me!

LISTEN
to the birds
sing
each
morning.
Their songs
send my
LOVE TO YOU

Prestigious Textiles

www.prestigious.co.uk
mail@prestigious.co.uk

83 // Prestigious Textiles was founded in 1988 by Trevor Helliwell and quickly carved out a niche as a specialist textile wholesaler and distributor. From their headquarters in the heartland of West Yorkshire, the company now supply retailers in the UK, Ireland and over 100 countries worldwide. Their portfolio of products includes fabrics for curtains, upholstery and accessories as well as wallpaper collections and curtain poles. Prestigious pride themselves on being able to forecast up-and-coming design trends and steer the trends themselves. For children they offer a wide-ranging collection of designs featuring cheerful colours, fun pictorial themes and coordinating prints.

Top / Home Sweet Home
(Lavender)
Colourful rows of houses
look perfect for a modern,
graphic girls' print.

Bottom / Escape (Vintage)
From Prestigious Textiles'
Ideal World collection.
Created to capture a child's
joy of travel through its naive
depictions of animals.

Opposite /
Mitsy Mouse (Linen)
From the Safari Park fabric
collection. Cute character
motifs such as mice and dogs
are filled with vibrant floral
and leaf patterns.

Rebecca Jones

thelittlestm.blogspot.com.au
rebeccajonesdesigns@gmail.com

84 // Rebecca Jones is originally from the UK where she studied for a BA (Hons) in Textiles and Fashion, specializing in print design, at the Winchester School of Art. After graduating, Rebecca went to work as a textile designer at John Lewis, and later for a design studio in London. Now based in Melbourne, Australia, Rebecca worked as a freelance designer for the first couple of years of motherhood for clients such as Marks & Spencer, Topshop, Anthropolgie, BabyGap, Pottery Barn, Zara and H&M. Rebecca currently works for a leading Australian speciality tablewares retailer, Adairs, where she says it is a privilege to be able to lead the design direction for the children's bedlinen and get first-hand feedback on the success of designs. Rebecca finds the online community is an endless source of inspiration, and creates many designs especially for her son, Toby. For the last few years Rebecca has been solely designing for tablewares, but in the future she would love to design quilting fabrics and move into illustration for children.

Design Heroes: Designers Guild (see pages 98–9), Olle Eksell, Shinzi Katoh

Favourite Children's Illustrators: Blanca Gómez (see pages 60–1), Marc Boutavant (see pages 196–9), Richard Scarry

Left / Chirpy Bird (Artwork)
The motifs of trees filled with
butterflies and flowers were
kept simple in this design,
and the colours were kept
pretty as it was created for
young girls. Designed for
Adairs Kids. © Copyright 2011
Adairs Retail Group.

Above / Chirpy Bird (Photo)
This design was created
for a large range of girls'
accessories, including
backpacks and lunch
bags, and was later used
for bedlinen and wall art.
Designed for Adairs Kids.
© Copyright 2011 Adairs
Retail Group.

Left / Candy Forest
Some of the heart-filled trees in this print have been made using a dashed stroke, which gives a light and airy feel. Designed to co-ordinate with the Bird Cameo design, it was printed on fabric via Spoonflower.

Above / Bird Cameo
Drawn digitally in Adobe Illustrator, this design was created for personal use. A series of decorative cameo frames filled with birds have been set against a tiny grid-patterned background. Rebecca was inspired by the many birds parading and strutting on her rooftop. It was printed on fabric via Spoonflower.

Robin & Mould

www.robinandmould.etsy.com
www.robinandmould.blogspot.com
robinandmould@googlemail.com

85 //   Amy Robinson and
Christian Mould are Robin & Mould.
Amy studied Graphic Design
at Nottingham Trent University
and Christian studied Fine Art at
the University of Wales Institute,
Cardiff. The couple are both
originally from Wiltshire and after
a few years away, living in London,
they recently returned. Robin
& Mould's designs are influenced
by Scandinavian design, children's
book illustration, architecture,
interiors, mid-century graphic
design, typography and nature.
Inspiration has also come from
becoming parents. They hadn't
yet started their business when
their first child was born and so
they were inspired to finally have
a go. Their 'Dream Big' design
comes from the very early days
of parenthood and the hopes
they had. They always ask Rufus
now what he thinks of a design
and if he can recognize what
it is, it gets his seal of approval.
Going forward, Amy and Christian
would love to design and print
fabric on a large scale, by the
metre, someday! They've also
always wanted to own their
own studio-come-shop, and
Christian would love to illustrate
a children's book.

Design Heroes: Saul Bass, Robin
and Lucienne Day, Stig Lindberg

Favourite Children's Illustrators:
Oliver Jeffers, Marc Boutavant
(see pages 196–9), Mary Blair

Top / Sleepy Dog Cushion
Inspired by Amy and
Christian's very own very
sleepy dog, this cute cushion
is hand screen-printed and
hand-sewn for sale on Etsy.
Patterns and motifs have
been added to the dog for
extra detailing.

Above / Dream Big Cushion
Designed after Amy and
Christian became parents
for the first time, this cushion
is hand screen-printed with
a beautiful handwritten script
on natural linen union using
water-based inks. It was
designed and handmade
to sell in the Robin & Mould
Etsy shop.

Top / Owl Cushions
(Teal, Yellow)
These shaped cushions are
hand screen-printed and
feature wings and feet that
are hand-cut from felt and
sewn before being attached.
Designed and handmade
to sell in the Robin & Mould
Etsy shop.

Left / Fox
A digital artwork featuring
a highly stylized illustration
of a fox. The mirrored
design uses two motifs
flipped to face different
directions. The design
has been used on screen-
printed cushions.

Above /
Fox Cushion (Back/Front)
The second in a possible
series of animal alphabet
cushions. This caption
appears on the reverse
with an image of a fox on
the other side. It was hand
screen-printed on natural
linen union using water-
based inks, for sale on Etsy.

Rosalind Maroney

www.rosalindmaroney.co.uk
wonder@rosalindmaroney.co.uk

86 // Rosalind Maroney is based in St Leonards-on-Sea, East Sussex. She studied for a BA (Hons) in Product Design at Central Saint Martins in London. Rosalind has designed for clients such as Harrods, John Lewis, Little Bird Told Me, Mamas & Papas, Mothercare and Narrative Studio. She says 'all sorts of everything' inspire her sketches and designs. Her ambition is to design more toy ranges and other products for children, mixing both product and textile design. Rosalind is a keen freelance designer up for any exciting opportunities that may arise – tablewares, stationery, her own product range – basically everything!

Design Heroes: Charley Harper, Lucienne Day, Jasper Morrison

Favourite Children's Illustrator: Elena Odriozola

BIGNESS CHART

TALL not Small

am i BIG yet?

= Big & STRONG

BIG

Left / Apple, Bear, Chair
This educational ABC design shows that colours for children's design don't have to be primary or rainbow based. A dark ground of crosshatch and a lime green chair set off this bear character nicely, and give it an eye-catching drama. Hand-drawn, then scanned and edited in Adobe Illustrator.

Above / am i BIG yet?
Some of the sketches are left hollow whilst others have pattern fills in this fabulous doodle-style design which was hand-drawn, scanned and edited in Adobe Illustrator. The message is put across with charm: water plus fruit and vegetables equals growing taller.

Ruka-Ruka

www.rukaruka.co.uk
info@rukaruka.co.uk

87 // Sinead Gray is originally from Ballyvaughan, in Ireland but is currently based in London. Sinead studied Visual Communication Design at Dun Laoghaire Institute of Art, Design, and Technology in Dublin. She started up Ruka-Ruka because she didn't want to go back to work at an agency while her children were small. She found inspiration for her designs from their inquisitiveness and inventiveness. Sinead's style influences have come from items such the Eames House of Cards, a series of pictures and patterns designed in 1952, and a handmade patchwork quilt. The beautifully illustrated storybooks given to her by her grandparents captivated her imagination as a child and still continue to inspire her today. Her philosophy is: 'We owe our children something more than a sea of garish plastic to feed their curiosity'.

Design Heroes: Alan Fletcher, Saul Bass, Paul Rand

Favourite Children's Illustrators: Leonard Weisgard, J.P. Miller, Ludwig Bemelmans

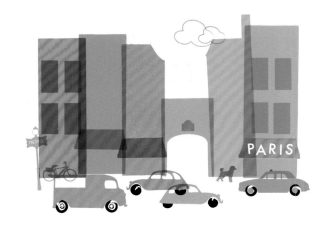

Top / Paris
Above / New York
Opposite top / London
Iconic cities have been depicted as chic retro prints to add colour and style to any child's room and fuel their imagination at the same time. Sinead has used transparent colours that overlap each other to create new colours. The prints can also be personalized with a name for christening, new baby or birthday gifts.

Opposite bottom / Circus Train
Circus designs were popular in the 1960s and nostalgic designs with a similar feel are still used today. This fine example was created as a children's decor art print and has lots of exuberant colour and movement from the swinging monkeys, a cloud of steam made from simple circles and an escaping transparent balloon.

Samarra Khaja

www.samarrakhaja.com
samarrakhaja.tumblr.com
info@samarrakhaja.com

88 // Samarra Khaja is half-Australian, half-Indian, was born in Canada and grew up all over the world. Samarra now lives in New York City where you will find her 'Heartbeat Brooklyn' mural; a large two-panelled public art piece that can be seen in Park Slope, Brooklyn. Samarra has a BFA in Fine Arts (Printmaking, Drawing and Photography). Her MFA work is in Photography. Clients have included *The New York Times,* Victoria's Secret, Bliss, Dyson, the American Museum of Natural History and New York University. She has always tried to approach her work with a sense of whimsy, exploration and discovery, and having her children around is a big influence that helps her to share their fresh view of the world. Other inspiration comes from city life, fashion, typography, thrift store and flea market finds, random pieces of history, childhood memories and world travel. Samarra also adores Scandinavian and Japanese design aesthetics and their ingenious melding of form and function. Her dream design commission would be to create an illustration for the MTA Arts for Transit subway art campaign in NYC, or she would be thrilled to design a postage stamp, for any country!

Design Heroes: Daphne Padden, Marimekko (see pages 204–7), Tom Eckersley

Favourite Children's Illustrators: Clare Mackie, Peter McCarty, Oliver Jeffers

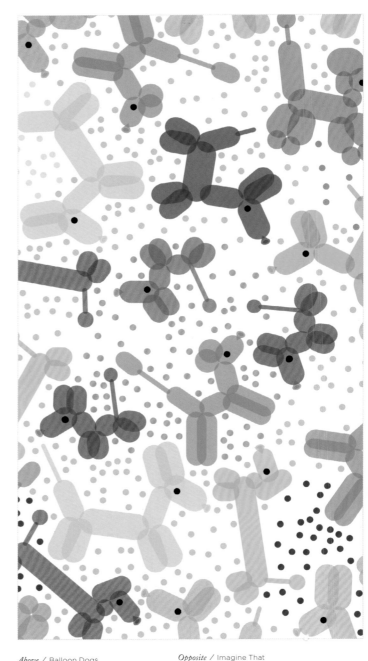

Above / Balloon Dogs
Celebrating a favourite magical childhood memory, Samarra created this piece initially for a Spoonflower textile design challenge, but it has since been released as part of her exclusive collection for Timeless Treasures. Created in Adobe Illustrator, it features cute sausage dogs made from transparent balloons and a scattering of tiny dots.

Opposite / Imagine That
Inspired by Spoonflower's 2011 Project Selvage textile design challenge. The travelling linework and spirit of Samarra's illustration were also inspired by a bedtime book called *Harold and the Purple Crayon,* which she read a lot at the time to her eldest son, Kip. All of the scenes were hand-drawn, scanned in, and coloured and assembled in Adobe Illustrator. It's now a part of her exclusive collection for Timeless Treasures.

Sarah Alcock

whistleandstitch.co.uk
sarah@whistleandstitch.co.uk

89 // Sarah Alcock is a designer from Manchester in the UK. Sarah studied Fashion and Textiles at Leicester Polytechnic and currently works as a freelance designer. She called her website Whistle and Stitch because she also loves to make things from upcycled fabric. Whilst working for manufacturers, Sarah designed prints for children's clothing, bedding, and products for companies such as Mothercare and Asda. Freelance clients include UK Greetings and Disney. Sarah finds inspiration everywhere and in everything, even in unexpected places like the supermarket. Having only recently turned freelance, design blogs have become a useful resource for Sarah. 'Bloggers have unknowingly become my invisible colleagues,' she says. Sarah had her first two children's stitch and collage books called *Who's Hiding in my Toybox? Robots* and *Who's Hiding in my Toybox? Animals* published in 2012 by Five Mile Press. Going forward she would love to illustrate another children's book and design for children's tableware. After several years in the industry, Sarah really hopes to become a successful freelance designer.

Design Heroes: Julie Arkell, Paper & Cloth, the Pop-i-Cok blog

Favourite Children's Illustrators: Lydia Monks, Delphine Durand, Paul Thurlby

Above /
Bird and Washi Tape Stripe
Japanese masking tape, known as washi tape, is a popular craft and decor trend that Sarah has been able to use in this cute print. Little birds sit on top of rows of tape pieces, making an effective striped design.

Opposite / Elephant and Bird
A charming elephant hands his bird friend a flower in this design, which would look great on stationery products. The bunting is a clever device for adding lots more colour and detail.

Notes

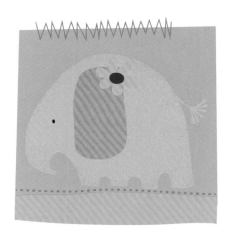

Opposite / Pen, Peep and Foxy
Little animal faces peep out from round discs which are overlaid on graph-style paper with postmarks. The softness of the colours and friendly faces are ideal for babies and toddlers.

Above / Hide and Peep traffic
This transport design is perfect for very small boys with its delicate drawings, pastel tone and super-sweet bears.

Sparky & Marie

www.sparkyandmarie.com
hello@sparkyandmarie.com

90 // Michelle Beilner is a graphic designer from Chicago who has worked for over a decade developing brands for a range of clients. Her studio Sparky & Marie was launched in 2010 and named after her beloved grandparents. Michelle studied Graphic Design at the University of Illinois and is now based in Los Angeles. Her inspiration comes from everyday living – especially flowers in the garden, colours from vintage finds and textures from nature walks. Michelle says she is very much in love with pop florals from the 1960s and '70s and this is often reflected in her work. For licensing enquiries Sparky & Marie is represented by MHS Licensing.

Design Heroes: Vera Neumann, Ray and Charles Eames, Marimekko (see pages 204–7)

Favourite Children's Illustrators: Eric Carle, Maurice Sendak, Mary Blair

Above / Sugar Blossom Fruits
Here Michelle has created a very pretty pattern from fruit and flower motifs. The apples and pears follow a diagonal line and the colour palette is very cute and appealing.

Opposite top / Mod Floral
A funky geometric floral design that has a mod flavour which would be ideal for girls' fashion or decor.

Opposite bottom left / Animal Parade
The animals in Michelle's parade have an almost sculptural quality. They are reduced to brightly coloured silhouetted shapes, whilst the detail comes from a tiny dotted ground and occasional use of polka dots. The striped structure would make it ideal for nursery cot bedding, curtains or lampshades.

Opposite bottom right / Rubber Ducky
The classic rubber duck has been depicted in a mix of solid colour and cross hatching on this bath-time pattern. The repeat is non-directional to give overall coverage.

Stephen Barker

www.felixhugo.com/seetree
stepenstep@aol.com
Agent: The Bright Agency

91 // Stephen Barker is originally from Stafford, UK, but is now based in Bristol where he studied Fine Art at the University of West England. Stephen is one of the artists represented by The Bright Agency and works as a freelance illustrator. He has illustrated children's books such as *Noah's Ark,* published by Caterpillar Books. Other clients have included Peaceable Kingdom Press, Campbell Books, Hotchpotch, Orchard Books and Lion Hudson. Stephen's main source of inspiration is nature and his dream commission would be to design an alphabet poster.

Design Heroes: Sol Linero, Raymond Savignac, Bellbug

Favourite Children's Illustrators: Marc Boutavant (see pages 196–9), Lydia Monks, Goolygooly

Top / Birthday Goats
A goat wearing a pink sweater and party hat is surrounded by cakes in a design that has a quirky charm. The illustration has the feel of being drawn with pastels or chalks. A mixed media artwork. © Stephen Barker – The Bright Agency.

Bottom / Birthday Birds
Birds at jaunty angles are lined up in birthday hats and armed with presents in this fun design. A mixed media artwork. © Stephen Barker – The Bright Agency.

Above / Hotchpotch Birthday Cards
A series of six card designs created for very young birthdays and published by Hotchpotch. Stephen's boldly illustrated animals are designed to attract the attention of little ones, with bright colours, strong shapes and appealing faces. A mixed media artwork.
© Stephen Barker – The Bright Agency. Design © Hotchpotch Publishing Ltd.

Studio 2

www.studio2art.com
work@studio2art.com

92 // Studio 2 is a creative partnership formed 15 years ago between Pattie Gaeta and Luci Rawding located in Wyckoff, New Jersey. The looks that Studio 2 offers are fun, bright, simple and graphic and they have created a growing collection of fresh designs ranging from whimsical-styled Santas to bright birthday graphics. Many of their creations are inspired by mid-century design as well as pop and contemporary art. Being located just outside New York City allows them to frequently visit museums and shop the fashion and home markets for style and colour trends. Their characters, for which they are best known, are inspired by the innocent, happy nature of children. They love to create designs that make people smile. Their dream project would be to write and illustrate a fun book to share the joy they have creating art and entertaining children of all ages.

Design Heroes: Alexander Girard, Andy Warhol, Milton Glaser

Favourite Children's Illustrators: Eric Carle, Paul Rand

Opposite / So Cute Placement
From Studio 2's modern quilt collection using graphic pattern fills to embellish the bold typography. Cute baby-friendly characters are dotted around the letters to make sure there are lots of friendly faces to connect with.

Top / Jungle Mobile Placement
Part of the Studio 2's Animal Crackers collection featuring simple silhouettes of baby animals with their sweet, sleepy expressions. This placement print cleverly uses the device of a traditional baby's mobile to anchor all the characters.

Bottom / Jungle Mobile Pattern
Here the jungle animal characters from the mobile are put into repeat in a tightly packed toss layout.

Studio Seed

www.studioseed.co.uk
hello@studioseed.co.uk

93 // Studio Seed was set up and is led by Tamsin Seed. Born and raised in rural Cheshire, Tamsin is currently located in a lovely pink studio in the West Midlands. She graduated from Manchester Metropolitan University with a degree in Embroidery, then went on to win two prestigious awards at the New Designers graduate exhibition in 2005. Tamsin worked her way up to become an in-house Senior Designer for Marks & Spencers' greetings, stationery and gifting ranges at Tigerprint. Since setting up her own business in 2010 Tamsin has worked with and sold work to clients including Gap Kids, Next, Debenhams, Designers Guild, Target Australia and Primark Kids. She is also represented by the fantastic Lemon Ribbon studio where Tamsin creates surface pattern and placement designs for baby and girlswear which are sold all over the world. Alongside children's design, Tamsin also designs and publishes greetings cards and wedding stationery. She is planning to further expand the stationery and greetings side of the business to include special children's ranges. A lot of Tamsin's print and pattern designs are inspired by her beautiful niece, Esmé, who reminds her to take joy and pleasure from the most simple things in life.

Design Heroes: Lisa Stickley, Jessica Hische, Oh! Joy

Favourite Children's Illustrators: Sara Fanelli, Jillian Phillips (see pages 156-9), Lisa Martin (see pages 180-3)

Above / Dreaming Girl
Tamsin created a sketch of a little girl character and added in the ditsy floral pattern. She loves to mix typographic styles and so used some hand-drawn lettering alongside a simple serif font for the text element. Created initially with stationery and greetings cards in mind, Tamsin can see this look working well for children's clothing as well.

Opposite /
Sketchy Ditsy Floral
The 'ditsy' mini-collection was inspired by Tamsin's original sketches of little florals and leaves. She took the sketches onto her Mac and added to the patterns there. Tamsin chose a modern, feminine but soft colour palette.

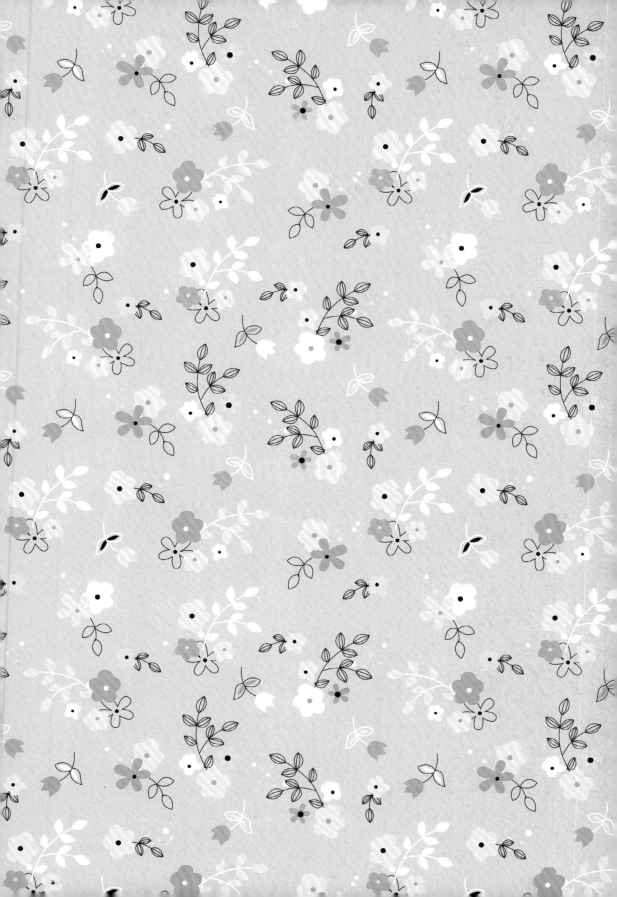

Susan Driscoll

www.theprinttree.com
theprinttree@yahoo.co.uk

94 // Susan Driscoll is based in Liverpool, where she designs freelance under her studio name, The Print Tree. Susan studied Printed Textile Design at Loughborough University and after graduating worked in New York designing prints for the fashion, home and stationery markets. Clients have included Ralph Lauren, Laura Ashley and Target. Susan finds inspiration in everything from nature to mid-century design, vintage textiles and contemporary illustration. Susan is open to all design opportunities and has exhibited at various trade fairs including Surtex, Printsource and Indigo. She has a dream wish-list of companies she would love to collaborate with in the future including Mamas and Papas, Anthropologie and Paperchase.

Design Heroes: Sonia Delaunay, Paul Smith, Atelier LZC

Favourite Children's Illustrators: Mandy Sutcliffe (see pages 54–7), Lauren Child

Left / Morning Tulip
A field of colourful spring
tulips cover this design,
which is densely packed
but harmonized by ensuring
all the flowers face the same
way up. Detail and interest
has been added by the
roughly scribbled hatching
effect on some of the
blooms. Created in Adobe
Photoshop using collage
and hand-drawn motifs
for Susan's portfolio.

Above / Butterflies in Spring
Created using both collage
and hand-drawn elements,
then digitally coloured
and repeated in Adobe
Photoshop. The butterflies
are made sharp and angular,
almost like bow ties, and
were inspired by the first
days of spring. Created for
Susan's portfolio.

Susan Mansell

susiemansell@gmail.com

95 // Susan Mansell is currently based in Bolton in the UK. She completed a Higher National Diploma in Surface Pattern Design at Cleveland College of Art & Design, where her love of embroidery first began, then graduated from Manchester Metropolitan University in 1991 with a degree in Embroidered Textiles. Susan's first job was 'punching' the embroidery discs for a UK nursery bedding manufacturer and she worked her way up to Design Manager. Her next job was at Lollipop Lane, where she helped create the brand and also worked on ranges for many high street stores. Susan enjoys working in the baby industry as she is passionate about creating cute, lovable characters with their own personalities and stories. She is inspired and influenced by blogs, magazines, children's books, childrenswear, the greetings card industry and by looking around the shops on a regular basis! Now working as a freelance designer, Susan mainly works for the nursery bedding market but would also love to enter the childrenswear and stationery market. She also has a love of painting and decorating so her dream design commission would be to combine the two and paint a children's nursery with her characters.

Design Heroes: William Morris, Tricia Guild (see pages 98–9), Alexander Girard

Favourite Children's Illustrators: Lauren Child, Lydia Monks, Dick Bruna

Opposite / Best Friends Forever (Pink & Blue)
A cot quilt design using cute, friendly characters created for Susan's portfolio using Adobe Illustrator. Designed to be printed with elements of embroidery and appliqué, with woven badge detailing. All Susan's designs originate from her sketchbook and, since she recently discovered the wonders of Adobe Illustrator, they are then recreated digitally.

Left / Over The Rainbow
A fun, unisex design for the junior bedding market. The bright, bold colours and cheerful characters depicting a garden scene were inspired by the colours of the rainbow. Hand-drawn then recreated in Adobe Illustrator.

Above / Tiptoe Teddy
Hand-drawn then recreated in Adobe Illustrator and Photoshop. Designed for Susan's portfolio for either baby bedding or clothing. Susan was wondering how this design could be reproduced as embroidery, so she created a stitch effect and used scanned buttons and fabrics to create a life-like quality. Hand-drawn lettering and fonts are combined as an integral part of the design.

Suzanne Washington

spellboundbydesign.wordpress.com
spellboundbydesign.blogspot.co.uk
suzyspellboundx@hotmail.com

96 // Suzanne Washington is based in Hinckley, Leicestershire. She studied Printed Textile design at Loughborough University College of Art and Design. Clients have included George clothing at Asda and several other UK high street clothing and homeware brands. Suzanne loves vintage nostalgia and museum curiosities. She draws inspiration from her own childhood, which was wonderful because her mother, Averil, would read to her every single night and really inspired her love of books, narrative and the magic of imagination. Today Suzanne enjoys visiting vintage fairs with her husband, Guy, who also has a great nostalgia for childhood toys and memorabilia. Suzanne would love to create cute characters for childrenswear and set up a vintage-inspired boutique baby and childrenswear label. Suzanne's mission statement is 'to create for the love of creating beautiful things', and she would be open to any projects that require original hand-drawn illustration and surface decoration.

Design Heroes: Rob Ryan, Cath Kidston (see pages 72-7), Paperchase (see pages 240-3)

Favourite Children's Illustrator: Beatrix Potter

Above / Sweet Garden
A summer print that is buzzing with insects and blooming with flowers. Suzanne created all the designs featured from self-directed moodboards and briefs. Created with girls' clothing in mind.

Top middle / Rise and Shine
A beautiful placement print created with girls' nightwear in mind and featuring a sweet little mouse waking up in a pretty flower pot.

Top right / Sleepy Woodland
Here Suzanne has created a whole collection of designs that work and blend together. There is a good mix of placement prints with cute woodland characters and supporting repeat patterns. The hibernating hedgehog makes them perfect for nightwear.

Opposite / Pet Alphabet
Adorable puppies with long, floppy ears feature on this boys' design that incorporates fun patchwork fills. All of Suzanne's work is created in Adobe Illustrator with hand-drawn elements and self-created patchwork fills.

E and
TINE

I'm not just
sleeping!
I'm
Hibernating

F is for fun...

Fun Friends and

friendship

getting to know you

is for
doggy

woof
woof woof

woof

Happy
doggy

go walkies?

nom nom
nom

WOOF
woof woof

woof

woof
woof

woof
woof

nom
nom
nom

woof
woof

woof
woof woof

WOOF

woof
woof woof

woof

nom
nom
nom

Vanja Kragulj

www.vanjakragulj.com
www.zoobabies.ca

97 // Vanja Kragulj was born in what is now known as Bosnia-Herzegovina. She moved to Canada in 1994 during the civil war and now lives in Montreal, Quebec, where she works as an illustrator and designer in the baby-product industry. Vanja has also developed her own children's brand called Zoo Babies, a collection of naive animal characters and their friends. So far the collection has expanded to include baby clothes, stationery, plush toys, wall art and wall decals. Vanja believes that her illustration work is really influenced by her graphic design background. As a result, her illustrations are both whimsical and graphic at the same time. She also loves colour and tends to use non-traditional colours for children, so her illustrations end up appealing to adults as well. Vanja recently gave birth to a baby boy and being a children's product consumer for the first time taught her about illustrating/designing for the consumer, while staying true to her own style and passion for children's illustration. She is certain that having a child will have a big influence on her future work and will hopefully make her a better designer.

Design Heroes: Sanna Annukka, Christiane Lemieux (Dwell Studio), Martha Stewart

Favourite Children's Illustrators: Marc Boutavant (see pages 196–9), Oliver Jeffers, Tarō Gomi

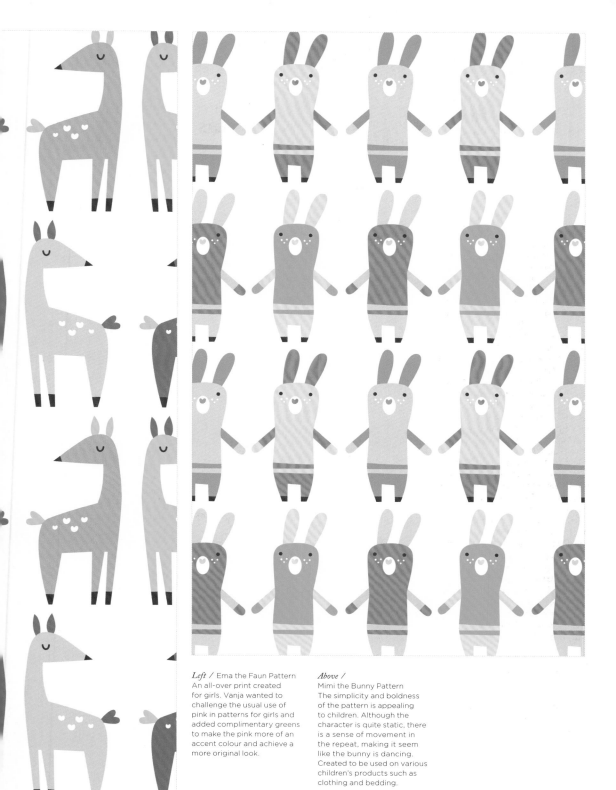

Left / Ema the Faun Pattern
An all-over print created
for girls. Vanja wanted to
challenge the usual use of
pink in patterns for girls and
added complimentary greens
to make the pink more of an
accent colour and achieve a
more original look.

Above /
Mimi the Bunny Pattern
The simplicity and boldness
of the pattern is appealing
to children. Although the
character is quite static, there
is a sense of movement in
the repeat, making it seem
like the bunny is dancing.
Created to be used on various
children's products such as
clothing and bedding.

Top left / Yuri the Bear
This image is part of a three-piece series featuring Yuri the Bear initially designed as wall art. Yuri was one of the original Zoo Babies characters that set the style for the whole range. The simplicity of the trees and the shape of the bear make them ideal for children's products. Currently sold as wall art and as a wall decal.

Top right / Heather the Owl
The pink colour palette and soft design elements are distinctly feminine, yet still graphic. The flowers are also reduced to basic shapes. Vanja chose not to use the soft pinks typically seen on baby girl products and instead paired the pink with a punchy peach and orange with complimentary green elements.

Bottom left / Edgar the Lion
This image was created to be printed on various children's products and is currently sold as wall art and as a wall decal. The colour palette is a combination of complimentary blues and oranges to appeal to both boys and girls.

Bottom right / Luka the Wolf
The colour palette, animal type and angular design elements here are more attractive to boys. The characterization of the wolf is very friendly and naive so the image is still appealing to children. Currently sold as wall art.

Opposite / Luka the Wolf Pattern
This is an all-over print created using Luka the Wolf from the Zoo Babies collection. The print has a crisp and clean graphic quality and was created to be used on various children's products such as children's clothing and bedding.

Victor Fox

www.foxyvictor.blogspot.com
www.etsy.com/shop/victorfox
foxyvictor@live.com

98 // Victor Fox is the studio name for designer Clare Westwood. Clare was born and raised in Geelong, Victoria, Australia, and started her studies for a degree in Graphic Design at Swinburne University, Melbourne, which she then finished at the Gordon Institute of Tafe, Geelong. Clare's clients have included Kaisercraft, Skip Hop and 41 Orchard (an Australian children's wall decal company). Clare is inspired by colour and simplicity. She loves fresh design and illustration, diamonds, triangles and shapes – anything bright and bold – and, of course, foxes! Clare's dream design commission would be to collaborate with or work for her favourite designer, Beci Orpin, or with Rachel Castle. 'They just amaze me!' she says. Clare likes to create new projects and make things such as clocks, jewellery, T-shirts, cards, swing tags, party bags, prints, sewing – whatever pops up in her mind.

Design Heroes: Angela Hardison, Darling Clementine, Beci Orpin

Favourite Children's Illustrator: Aliki

All designs from the Fine & Sunny range – a scrapbooking/craft paper collection designed for Kaisercraft. This included six double-sided papers with matching embellishments. All elements in the range were hand-drawn and then constructed on the computer.
www.kaisercraft.com.au

Top left / Sunshower
All the elements of the Fine & Sunny collection are brought together in one busy design.

Top right / Avenue
Rows of little buildings give a structured stripe look to this 30 x 30cm (12 x 12 inch) paper design. A scalloped stripe forms the division between each street.

Bottom left / Fine & Sunny
The logo for the Fine & Sunny collection is used to brand the marketing materials.

Bottom right / Sky
A scalloped border is an echo from the Avenue design and forms a frame around this paper, with motifs in opposite corners to allow the scrapbooker room to do their work.

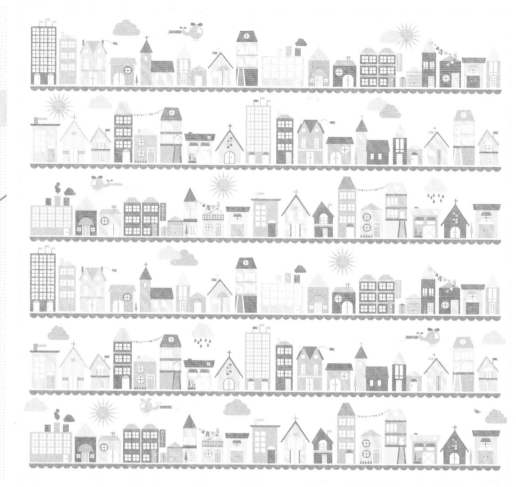

We Love Patterns

www.welovepatterns.com
gaston.caba@welovepatterns.com

99 // We Love Patterns is a family company created in 2010 by Gastón Caba. Gastón is originally from Patagonia, but is now based in Buenos Aires, Argentina, where he studied Graphic Design at the Universidad de Buenos Aires. Gastón has been working as a fashion illustrator since 2001, creating works for clients such as Adidas, Diesel, Benetton, Kappa and Sony Playstation. Since 2010 Gastón has been running We Love Patterns, who create, license and sell original artwork for products. He is also devoted to teaching and regularly gives workshops about illustrated pattern design in South America. Gastón is inspired by animals, mushrooms and silly things.

Design Heroes: Josef Frank, Gunta Stölzl, Mina Perhonen

Favourite Children's Illustrators: Tomi Ungerer, Wilhelm Busch, Meg Rutherford

Left / Cats, Dogs and Rabbits in Space
Space, rockets and planets are a popular theme for boys, and here they are given the cute Gastón treatment.

Top /
Cats, Dogs and Rabbits Driving Delivery Trucks
Animals deliver their favourite foods via truck, adding humour and whimsy to this striped design.

Bottom /
Cats, Dogs, Rabbits, Flowers and Mushrooms
Large, oversized heads and little, soft bodies make these characters full of fun and charm. All of the designs featured are from the We Love Patterns Animal Wallpaper series.

Above / Astronaut Cats and Stars
A little cat astronaut floats in space in this cute print suitable
for all kinds of children's products.

Opposite / Cats and Dogs Under Umbrellas
As Gaston says, We Love Patterns specialize in the 'extra cute'.
These cat and dog vignettes have been very cleverly framed
by the rainfall.

Wendy Burns

wendysdesignblog.blogspot.co.uk
wendyd.burns@btinternet.com

100 // Wendy Burns is originally from Lichfield in Staffordshire, but now works as a freelance designer in Nottingham. Wendy studied Textiles at Loughborough College of Art and Design. She currently works predominately in the childrenswear market for retailers from George at Asda and TU Clothing to The White Company. Wendy also works with numerous suppliers and manufacturers, and when she has time she loves working on her own range of designs. She is currently represented by Lemon Ribbon. Her greatest influence has to be her two children – her son's wild imagination has been an inspiration for many characters. Her daughter's love of fashion and all things vintage has broadened her horizons, and kept her up-to-date with blogging and trends, and therefore given her opportunities to showcase her work. Although Wendy's work is predominately digital-based, she still loves to retain that hand-drawn/sewn feel, which was her original foundation. Future dreams are to take her work into children's illustrations and to one day have the opportunity to bring her characters to life through animation.

Design Heroes: Rob Ryan, Cath Kidston (see pages 72–7), Orla Kiely (see pages 232–3)

Favourite Children's Illustrators: Mick Inkpen, Nick Sharratt, Eric Carle

Above / Cute Cat
Artwork mixing hand-drawn and stamp fonts. The simple spots and stripes make a fun print for younger girls.

Top right / Flower Girl
Along with a selection of co-ordinating prints, this little girl is richly detailed with flowers in her hair and patterns on her dress. Created for Wendy's agent, Lemon Ribbon.

Bottom left / Magical Dream Garden
An enchanting combination of flat colour with sketchy linear doodles to create a vibrant print for toddler girls. Commissioned by TU at Sainsbury's. Reproduced by kind permission of Sainsbury's Supermarkets Ltd.

Bottom right / Summer Bike Ride
Overflowing with pretty florals, this T-shirt placement includes elements of appliqué and embroidery commissioned by TU at Sainsbury's. Reproduced by kind permission of Sainsbury's Supermarkets Ltd.

Overleaf / Summer Flowers
This co-ordinating floral print creates an explosion of colourful blossom that is both delicate and fun, for young girls.

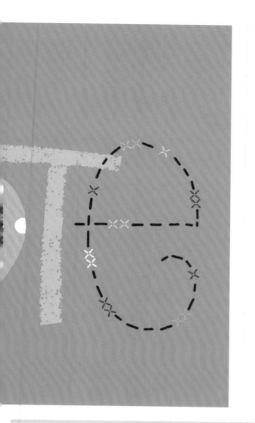

Westfalenstoffe

www.westfalenstoffe.de
info@westfalenstoffe.de

101 // Westfalenstoffe is a traditional, family owned business that has been creating beautiful fabrics in Germany for generations. In Germany, fairy tales are beloved and are a part of the culture even today. It was in honour of the 200th anniversary of the Brothers Grimm that Westfalenstoffe asked designer Rebekah Ginda to create a Fairy Tale collection for them. The fabric collection includes favourite stories such as Cinderella, Snow White, Sleeping Beauty, Hansel & Gretel, Little Red Riding Hood and Bremen Town Musicians. As Westfalenstoffe still produce designs that have been in production since the 1930s, it was important that the designs had a timeless feel. The brief was to create prints with a retro vibe, but in a fresh way and using fun colours.

Right / Rotkäppchen
(Little Red Riding Hood)
As this is such a forest based story Rebekah wanted to give this print a folky feel. The natural forms of trees create the dark shape of the woods and give the layout great structure.

Opposite / Bremer Stadtmusikanten
(Bremen Town Musicians)
In this print animals are playing music outside of a lit cottage, where robbers are inside counting their loot. To make a pleasing arrangement Rebekah cleverly designed the musical farm animals into a stack performing on top of one another.

Overleaf /
Prinzessinnen (Princesses)
Rebekah designed this pattern to incorporate some of the most beloved fairy tale princesses – Rapunzel, Cinderella, Sleeping Beauty and Snow White. Created with a combination of hand sketching and digital sketching.

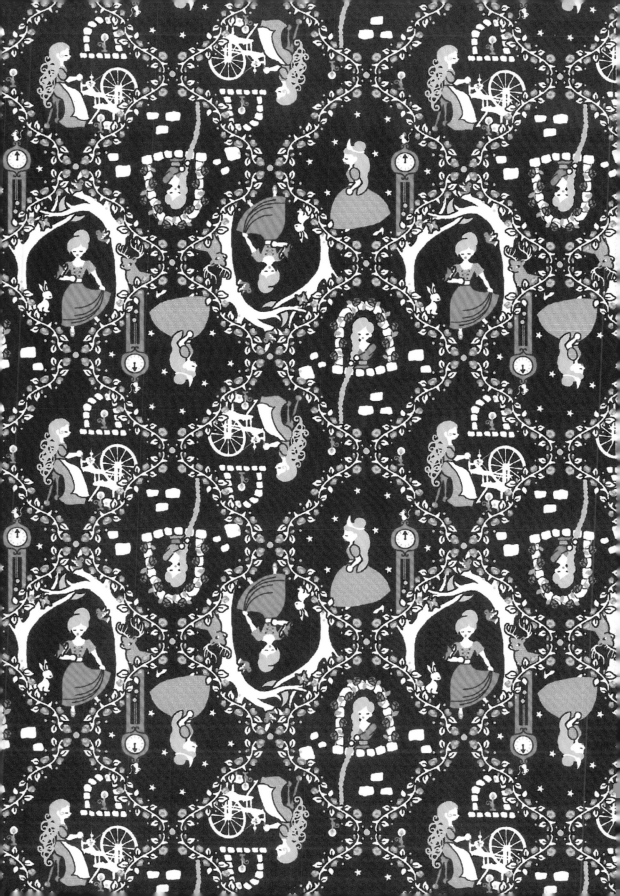

Zutano

www.zutano.com
customerservice@zutano.com

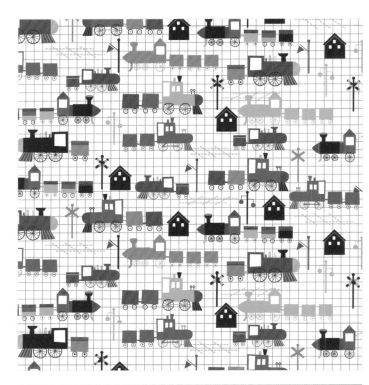

102 // Zutano is an internationally distributed children's clothing, accessories and plush toy company based in the US. The company was inspired by the birth of a baby daughter to Uli and Michael Belenky. Feeling uninspired by the children's clothing available to new parents, they founded Zutano in 1988 from their New York City apartment. The name Zutano was taken from the last word in a Spanish dictionary. Over 20 years later, and now based in the green hills of Vermont, Zutano are still producing beautiful babies' clothes for ages ranging from tiny newborns to growing toddlers. In more recent years they have begun designing children's bedding and nursery decor. They are known for their use of colour and graphic prints, where themes include family, travel, healthy and delicious food, nature and music. They also like to ensure prints can happily mix and match with carefully selected graphics, colours, stripes and geometrics, many of which are designed by Zutano's co-founder, Uli. As Zutano say, 'Our inspiration was, and will always be, babies.'

Top / Locomotive
Repeat pattern. Simple graphic blocks make up the shapes of the trains, contrasting beautifully with the more delicate spoked wheels, all set against a grid pattern suggesting graph paper.

Above / Choo Choo
T-shirt placement print. A strong graphic print for boys featuring a variety of typefaces designed to co-ordinate with the Locomotive pattern.

Top left / Garden Snail
Repeat pattern. A busy
design representing a
colourful garden that is full
of life. The snails provide
a friendly, smiling face and
the butterflies give the
design movement.

Top right / Snail
T-shirt placement print.
In picking out characters
from the Garden Snail
pattern, just the right
balance has been achieved
in this layout: flowers
for structure, butterflies
for action and the snail
for character.

Left / Mushroom
A fun print featuring
colourful mushrooms
whose caps are filled with
spots to give the design
some texture.

Opposite / Beluga
Repeat Pattern. A cute
whale print featuring
friendly and appealing
ocean creatures, perfect
for summer at the beach.

Above / Ship Ahoy
T-shirt placement print.
An ideal print for boys,
capturing the mood of
the ships and the coast in
a fun and lively illustration.

Acknowledgements

Huge thanks to:
All the designers, studios, companies
and artists who gave their beautiful
work to create this book; all the
readers and sponsors of the Print
& Pattern website who find it useful
and make it worthwhile; Helen
Rochester for recognizing our
genre as a separate discipline and
commissioning the Print & Pattern
series of books; Sophie Wise and
Sarah Batten for keeping it all in
check at Laurence King; Jordan
Nelson at & SMITH for the wonderful
layouts and design.

Thank you to Mum, Dad, Mark
and Lisa for all their support and
encouragement.